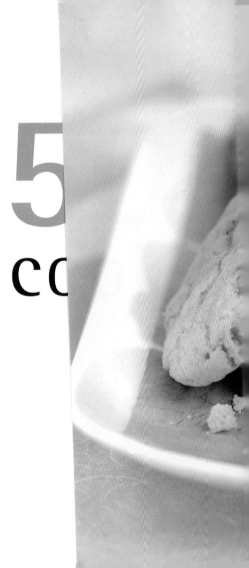

5
CO

500
cookies

the only cookie compendium you'll ever need

Philippa Vanstone

with an introduction by Susannah Blake

RONNIE
SELLERS
PRODUCTIONS
PORTLAND, MAINE

A Quintet Book

Published by Ronnie Sellers Productions, Inc.
P.O. Box 818, Portland, Maine 04104
For ordering information:
(800) 625-3386 Toll Free
(207) 772-6814 Fax
Visit our Web site: www.rsvp.com • E-mail: rsp@rsvp.com

President and Publisher: Ronnie Sellers
Publishing Director: Robin Haywood
Production Editor: Mary Baldwin
Associate Editor: Jessica Curran

ISBN: 1-56906-592-6

This book was designed and produced by
Quintet Publishing Limited
6 Blundell Street
London N7 9BH

Project Editor: Jenny Doubt
Editor: Ruth Patrick
Art Director: Roland Codd
Photography: Ian Garlick
Stylist: Susannah Blake
Home Economist: Fergal Connelly
Publisher: Ian Castello Cortes

10 9 8 7 6 5 4 3 2 1

Manufactured in Singapore by Pica Digital Pte Ltd.
Printed in China by SNP Leefung Printers Ltd.

contents

introduction

Susannah Blake

The modern-day cookie is said to be an American invention, although versions of these sweet confections can be found throughout the world, with every country boasting its own speciality. The earliest cookies can be traced back centuries — the Romans made a cookie consisting of a pasta-like dough that was fried and served with honey, while other cookies have been traced back to 7th century Persia, one of the first countries to cultivate sugar.

The term "cookie" was first used in the United States, and is derived from *koekje*, the Dutch word for the little cakes that were brought to New York by early settlers. However, generations of immigrants from Germany, Eastern Europe, Scandinavia, England, Scotland, and Ireland have also made their mark on the history of the cookie.

the earliest cookies

The largely British term "biscuit" is derived from the Latin *panis biscoctus*, meaning "bread twice-cooked." These savory Roman biscuits were baked twice to dry out, giving them a longer life, thus making them ideal for feeding armies and travelers. Sweet cookies such as German *zwieback*, Jewish *Mandelbrot*, and Italian *biscotti* and *cantucci*, which are all twice-baked, undoubtedly evolved from these early biscuits.

Pretzels date back thousands of years. They were invented by monks in a monastery in France where they were used to symbolize the marriage bond. The twisted strands of dough have also been said to symbolize a child's arms folded in prayer; the holes are the holy trinity.

Gingerbread is thought to have been first baked in Europe at the end of the 11th century, after crusaders introduced the ginger root. It later became a specialty of Medieval Germany, and by the 17th century, gingerbread baking was recognized as a profession whereby only professional gingerbread makers were allowed to bake the spicy confection. It was also in Medieval Germany that the tradition of crafting cookie dough into shapes at Christmas became a tradition. However, the first gingerbread "men" are credited to the court of Elizabeth I of England, where important visitors were favored with a gingerbread likeness of themselves. Gingerbread houses appeared in Germany in the early 19th century after the brothers Grimm published their first collection of fairytales, which included the story of Hansel and Gretel.

Recipes for shortbread and shortcake have been popular since the 16th century. Petticoat tails, the classic shortbread baked in a round and marked into wedges, resembles a crinoline petticoat and is thought to date back to the 12th century. The American butter cookie bears a strong resemblance to this traditional shortbread.

Cookies made of whisked egg whites and ground nuts have been popular since the Middle Ages, and eventually evolved into today's macaroon-type cookies. Furthermore, the discovery that beaten egg aerates cookie mixtures and gives them a lighter texture, lead to the evolution of sponge biscuits, boudoir biscuits, Lisbon biscuits, and Naples biscuits.

During the 19th century sugar, flour, and chemical raising agents such as baking soda became readily available and affordable, leading to the development of many sweet cookie recipes. Industrialization then made the manufacture of cookies in factories possible, beckoning in the era of mass-produced cookies. These cookies today are found in bite-size shapes, as traybakes cut into squares and bars, or as giant cookies that are served like cake; they can be served plain, dusted with sugar, coated in chocolate, spread with icing, drizzled with glaze, decorated with candy, or sandwiched with a rich creamy filling. Whatever your taste, you'll find them all here to bake — straight from your kitchen.

advice for readers

how to use this book
Each of the chapters in this book is comprised of two sections: a series of base recipes and a number of variations on each of the base recipes. With a slight modification of the original recipe, the addition of a cup of raisins or substitution of melted chocolate for white chocolate chips for example, you can create a host of new and exciting cookies.

wrapping, serving, & storing
We have suggested that parchment paper (or waxed paper) be used to wrap dough and line standard baking sheets where a non-stick baking sheet is not available. Plastic wrap can also be used to wrap dough that requires refrigerating. Foil is recommended for dough that needs to be wrapped and refrigerated in a specific shape. Serving and storage information is indicated at the end of each recipe — though please note that these are only approximates.

sugar, eggs, & chocolate
Unless the recipe indicates that eggs should be beaten, combine them into the recipe whole. When recipes call for brown sugar, ensure that you pack the sugar when measuring it out in order that the correct amount is used. Finally, we recommend that unrefined sugar be used in recipes contained in the *wholesome healthy cookies* chapter, as this chapter is comprised of recipes whose ingredients offer healthier options. Replace bittersweet, semisweet, and milk chocolate according to taste.

refrigerated vs fresh dough
If cooking from refrigerated dough, preheat the oven to the temperature indicated 15 minutes before you want to bake the prepared cookie dough.

equipment

You only need a few basic pieces of equipment to make most cookies.

scales, measuring jugs, cups, & spoons
Baking is an exact science, so correct measuring equipment is essential. If the proportions of ingredients are incorrect, the recipe may not work, so always use accurate weighing scales and calibrated measuring jugs and cups, and proper measuring spoons.

mixing bowls & spoons
You will need a large bowl and wooden spoon for mixing most doughs. Small-sized bowls are useful for melting butter or chocolate or for mixing small quantities such as icing. A large metal spoon is useful for folding ingredients into delicate mixtures.

sieves
You will need a large sieve for sifting dry ingredients such as flour and a small sieve for dusting icing sugar or cocoa powder over baked cookies.

rolling pins
Useful for making rolled cookies, although you can use a straight-sided bottle instead. Mini rolling pins are easy for children to use.

cookie cutters
You can cut out rolled cookie dough by hand using a sharp knife, though it is much easier to use cookie cutters. They are available in all shapes and sizes, including rounds, hearts, stars, and Christmas trees.

baking sheets & pans
Most cookies are best baked on a flat baking sheet – the flat shape allows air to circulate around the cookies. Baking trays, which have a lip around all four sides, can also be used.

palette knives & metal spatulas
Useful for transferring uncooked rolled cookies onto baking sheets, or transferring baked cookies to a wire rack. Small palette knives are good for spreading cookies with filling or icing.

timers
When baking cookies, timing is crucial, so it's advisable to always use a timer. Accurate digital timers are inexpensive, and well worth the investment.

wire racks
After baking, most cookies should be transferred to a wire rack to cool.

piping bags
Piping bags and nozzles are useful for making piped cookies as well as for decorating baked cookies. For piping icing and melted chocolate, you can usually use a small plastic bag with the corner snipped off.

other equipment
Electric mixers can be great time-savers for mixing cookie doughs and can be bought quite inexpensively. A whisk is essential for whisking egg whites, and helpful for removing lumps from mixtures. Marble pastry boards can be useful for rolling out cookie dough.

ingredients

Most cookies are made using three basic ingredients: butter, sugar, and flour, with the frequent addition of other ingredients such as eggs, chocolate, nuts, and vanilla.

butter & other fats

Sweet butter is usually best for cookie-making. For cut-in cookie mixtures, use cold, firm butter; for creamed mixtures, use butter at room temperature; for melted mixtures, dice the butter before gently warming. White cooking fats and mild-tasting vegetable oils are also used instead of butter, and are a good choice for those with an intolerance or allergy.

sugar & other sweeteners

Different sugars add their own unique taste and texture to cookies. Refined white sugars add sweetness, while unrefined brown sugars add flavor. The texture of the sugar will also affect the cookie. Superfine sugar is most frequently used for cookie-making because it combines well with butter, but granulated sugar and coarse-textured sugars such as raw sugar and moist sugars such as molasses sugar are also used. Confectioners' sugar is generally used for dusting cookies and making icing. Light corn syrup, maple syrup, honey, and molasses can also be used in cookies, either in place of, or alongside, sugar.

flour & flour alternatives

Most cookies are made with plain flour, or self-rising flour — this gives them a lighter texture. Whole-wheat flour is sometimes used, but produces cookies with a heavy, dense texture. Non-wheat flours, often combined with wheat flour, can also be used. These include cornmeal, oatmeal, cornstarch, and rice flour. Rolled oats and ground nuts are common alternatives to flour.

eggs

These enrich cookie mixtures and bind ingredients together. For the best results, use eggs at room temperature. When whisking egg whites, be sure to use a clean, grease-free bowl.

other ingredients & flavorings

Dried fruits, such as raisins, sultanas, apricots, and cranberries are a popular addition to cookie mixtures. They are naturally sweet, so you may be able to use less sugar in the actual cookie mixture. Different dried fruits are often interchangeable in recipes.

Nuts are another popular addition, either whole, chopped, slivered, or ground. They add texture, and flavor.

Seeds such as sunflower, sesame, and poppy are often stirred into basic cookie doughs, particularly wholesome and savory cookie doughs.

Chocolate is widely used in cookie-making, usually as a flavoring, but also as a topping, and sometimes as a binding ingredient. Cocoa powder can be stirred into basic cookie doughs, or used to dust baked cookies. Chocolate chips can be stirred into mixtures, and plain, milk, or white chocolate can be melted and stirred into mixtures, or used to coat or decorate baked cookies.

Royal icing — a combination of confectioners' sugar, egg whites, and lemon juice that hardens when dry and can be varied using food coloring — is often used for decorating baked cookies. Chocolate-hazelnut spread and lemon curd, a creamy mixture made from juice, sugar, butter, and egg yolks, are both popular toppings, and are also used to sandwich filled cookies together.

Other cookie flavorings include spices, herbs, vanilla, coffee, citrus zest, almond extract, and orange extract.

making cookies

With all the hundreds of different cookies in the world, there are still only five main types of mixture: creamed, cut-in, melted, whisked, and all-in-one. These mixtures can then be used to make eight different types of cookies.

Creamed mixtures are made with soft butter beaten with sugar until fluffy, then blended with flour, eggs, and other ingredients. Creamed cookies include classic butter cookies.

Cut-in mixtures are made with cold, firm butter, which is cut into the flour, then bound together with eggs, milk, or another liquid. Viennese pockets are one of the classic cookies made using the cut-in method.

Melted mixtures are made of butter melted with sugar or syrup, and combined with dry ingredients. Classic melted cookies include flapjacks or gingerbread.

Whisked mixtures are made of whisked eggs and sugar (or a meringue mixture), into which the dry ingredients are folded. Classic whisked cookies include macaroons.

All-in-one mixtures are made by putting all the ingredients in a bowl and beating them together. These cookies can usually be made in a food processor, with any chunky ingredients such as dried fruit or nuts stirred in at the last minute.

drop cookies
Made with a soft creamed or all-in-one mixture, drop cookies are made by dropping spoonfuls of cookie mixture onto a baking sheet. They can be soft or firm, and are usually thick. Drop cookies can also be made using melted mixtures. The mixture usually spreads out on the baking sheet and results in large, flat, thin, crisp cookies. Melted drop cookies are often pliable when they come out of the oven and can be shaped while warm — either rolled around a wooden spoon handle to make tubes, draped over a rolling pin to make curls, or molded over a foil-covered orange to make a basket.

rolled cookies

Made with a firm cookie dough that can be rolled out on a floured surface, these cookies can be made with a creamed, melted, or cut-in mixture, which is usually chilled before rolling out. They're great for making with children, who will enjoy cutting shapes out of the dough with cookie cutters.

Rolled doughs are also great for making into multi-colored cookies. Divide the dough into two pieces before chilling, and knead a few drops of food coloring or 1 tablespoon unsweetened cocoa into half the dough. Chill, then roll out the two different doughs to equal thickness. Using a large cookie cutter, cut out cookies from each sheet of dough and then, using a smaller cutter, cut out the inside of the cookies. Carefully swap over the cookie centers so that each cookie has a different colored middle.

Alternatively, make spiral-patterned cookies. Brush the sheet of plain rolled dough with egg white and lay the colored sheet of dough on top. Roll up tightly to make a log, then slice the dough to make swirly cookies.

piped cookies

Usually made with soft creamed mixtures that are soft enough to press through a piping bag, piped cookies may also be made with whisked mixtures. Piping gives them a professional look, and also makes them very quick and easy to shape. Popular shapes include rosettes, swirls, and fingers.

shaped cookies

Firm doughs can be shaped using molds or baking pans, or by rolling bite-sized pieces of dough into balls or thin fingers. Fingers of dough can then be shaped into twists or knots.

Classic molded cookies include shortbread, for which special molds are available, while hand-shaped cookies include pretzels and lovers' knots.

cookie bars & traybakes

Most often based on creamed, cut-in, or melted mixtures baked in a baking pan, these cookies can vary enormously in shape, size, and texture. Usually cut into squares, bars, fingers, or wedges, they can be soft and moist, sticky and chewy, or firm and crisp. Cookie bars are often layered with a cookie base and an indulgent topping. Classic cookie bars include blondies, flapjacks, and the multi-layered millionaire's shortbread.

icebox cookies

The dough for these cookies can be stored in the refrigerator for one to two weeks, so you can make a few freshly baked cookies at a time, or just prepare the dough in advance to save time later. The dough is usually firm, made from creamed, cut-in, or melted mixtures, and can be kept in a container and scooped onto a baking tray or shaped into balls. Alternatively, it may be rolled into a log shape, wrapped in clear film or parchment, and then sliced into cookies when you're ready to bake.

no-bake cookies

Rather than baking, these cookies are set by chilling or cooling. Dry ingredients such as broken cookies, breakfast cereal, nuts, dried fruit, and marshmallows are stirred into a melted mixture — usually a combination of butter, chocolate, or syrup — then pressed into a mold or baking pan and cooled until set.

baking, cooling, & storing

Different types of cookies need to be baked at different temperatures, so always follow the recipe instructions. Cookie bars are usually cooked in a low to moderate oven (between 325°F [160°C] and 350°F [180°C]). Drop cookies are usually baked in a moderate oven (about 350°F [180°C]) to allow them to spread while they cook, crisping them on the outside while retaining a moist, chewy center. Rolled, piped, and icebox cookies are usually cooked in a moderate to hot oven (between 350°F [180°C] and 400°F [200°C]). Some cookies such as biscotti and cantucci are baked twice, first as a loaf of dough, which is then sliced and the individual cookies are returned to the oven to crisp up.

Oven temperatures tend to vary from model to model so always check the cookies a couple of minutes before their baking time is up to avoid over-cooking. The temperature within the oven can also vary, so move the baking sheets around part way through cooking to ensure even cooking. Never bake more than two sheets of cookies at a time because it may cause the oven temperature to drop.

Cookies baked on a baking sheet should usually be left to firm up for a few minutes, before transferring to a wire rack to cool. This allows air to circulate around the cookies and prevents warm moisture condensing and making the cookies soggy. Cookie bars are usually best left to cool in the pan before cutting into pieces and removing — although placing the baking pan on a wire rack will help to speed up the cooling process.

Most cookies are best eaten straight from the oven, but they also store well. As soon as the cookies are cool, pack them into an airtight container. This will help to keep soft cookies moist, and dry cookies crisp. Unfilled and undecorated cookies can also be frozen. Freeze in a single layer on baking sheets, and transfer to an airtight container and freeze until required. To thaw, transfer to a wire rack and leave at room temperature for about 30 minutes

classic cookies

These are the cookies and bars that have been
sampled and loved for decades — from peanut
butter cookies to tollhouse bars, and from biscotti
to the legendary neiman marcus chocolate chip
cookie. These are the simple essentials to any
cookie-maker's repertoire.

scottish shortbread

see variations page 41

Buttery, crumbly, and simple to make — you'll love this version of classic shortbread. You can use the recipe to make cookies, or as a base for cheesecakes or other desserts.

1½ cup all-purpose flour
2 tbsp. rice flour
¾ cup (1½ sticks) sweet butter

½ cup superfine sugar
2 tsp. vanilla extract
2 tsp. granulated sugar

Preheat the oven to 300°F (150°C). Line a 7 x 11-in. (18 x 28-cm.) pan with foil. Sift the all-purpose flour into a large bowl and add the rice flour.

Beat the butter and the superfine sugar until smooth. Add the vanilla extract and stir in the granulated sugar. Work the dough until it starts to clump together, then press it into the pan.

Bake for 45 to 50 minutes. The shortbread will look cooked before it actually is, so ensure that it bakes for the full 45 minutes.

Remove from the oven, sprinkle with extra granulated sugar, and cut into fingers. Cool for 20 minutes and remove from the pan.

Store in an airtight container for up to 5 days.

Makes 1½ dozen

almond biscotti

see variations page 42

This twice-baked Italian biscuit can be enjoyed with coffee or served with sorbet as a dessert.

2 cups all-purpose flour
1 cup superfine sugar
1 tsp. baking powder
¼ tsp. salt

3 eggs
2 tsp. vanilla extract
1 cup (5 oz.) whole blanched almonds

Preheat the oven to 300°F (150°C). Grease and flour 2 baking sheets. Mix the dry ingredients together in a large bowl. Whisk the eggs and vanilla extract together then stir into the dry ingredients. Add the almonds and stir them into the dough. The dough should be sticky.

Divide the dough between the baking sheets and shape into 2 flat loaves about 10 in. (25 cm.) long and 2 in. (5 cm.) wide. Bake for 35 to 40 minutes until pale golden. Remove from the oven onto a chopping board and immediately slice into thin pieces about ½ in. (1 cm.) wide.

Lay the slices back onto the baking sheets and cook for 10 to 15 minutes. Turn over each slice and cook for a further 10 to 15 minutes, or until the slices are golden brown. Remove from the oven and allow to cool.

When cool, store in an airtight container. The biscotti will keep for a couple of weeks.

Makes 3½ dozen

peanut butter cookies

see variations page 43

Rich and creamy, these cookies are a real indulgence for peanut butter fans.

1½ cups all-purpose flour
½ tsp. baking soda
½ cup (1 stick) sweet butter
½ cup superfine sugar

½ cup unrefined light brown sugar
1 egg
1 cup (8 oz.) crunchy peanut butter
Pinch of salt

Sift the flour and baking soda together. In a separate bowl, beat the butter and sugars until soft and creamy. Combine the egg, flour mixture, peanut butter, and salt. Add the butter and sugar mixture and mix until smooth.

Wrap the dough in foil or parchment and refrigerate for at least 2 hours, preferably overnight.

Preheat the oven to 325°F (160°C).

Shape the dough into 1¼-in. (3-cm.) balls and place them 2 in. (5 cm.) apart on baking sheets. Flatten slightly with a fork. Bake 15 minutes, or until golden.

Remove from the oven and allow to cool. Store in an airtight container for up to 5 days.

Makes 2 dozen

ginger nuts

see variations page 44

Crunchy and spicy, these sugar-crusted cookies are a sophisticated cookie treat.

¼ cup (½ stick) sweet butter, melted and cooled
2 tbsp. molasses
½ cup unrefined dark brown sugar
1 egg
1 cup all-purpose flour

1 tsp. baking soda
1 tsp. ground ginger
¼ tsp. ground allspice
Granulated sugar, to decorate

Preheat the oven to 350°F (175°C). Mix the cooled melted butter, molasses, unrefined dark brown sugar, and egg in a large bowl. Sift the remaining dry ingredients together and stir into the butter mixture.

Using about 1½ tablespoons of dough at a time, form the dough into balls. Place the balls 2 in. (5 cm.) apart on a non-stick baking sheet or use parchment on a standard baking sheet. Lightly press the cookies into 1¼-in. (3-cm.) rounds.

Refrigerate the cookies for 1 hour before baking. Sprinkle with granulated sugar and bake for 10 to 12 minutes. The cookies will puff up, then settle when cooked. Transfer the cookies to a wire rack to cool. Store in an airtight container for up to 5 days.

Makes 1½ dozen

linzer cookies

see variations page 45

These cookies originated from the sweet pastry used to make Austria's Linzer tart.

1 cup (5 oz.) roasted skinned hazelnuts
2 cups all-purpose flour
½ cup granulated sugar
¼ tsp. salt
2 tsp. ground cinnamon

¼ tsp. ground cloves
1 cup (2 sticks) sweet butter
Grated zest of 1 lemon (2 to 3 tsp.)
¼ cup raspberry jelly
2 tbsp. confectioners' sugar

Preheat the oven to 350°F (175°C). Grind the hazelnuts in a food processor until fine. Add the flour, granulated sugar, salt, cinnamon, cloves, and butter to the food processor and pulse until the mixture looks crumbly. Add the lemon and pulse until the mixture clumps together.

Work the dough into a flat round shape, wrap in parchment, and refrigerate for 30 minutes, or until firm. On a floured surface, roll out the dough to ⅛ in. (3 mm.) thick. Using a cookie cutter, cut out shapes, ensuring you have equal numbers of each shape. Place half the cookies on parchment-lined baking sheets and cut out a hole in each center. Bake the cookies with the cut-out centers separately from the remaining cookies for 8 to 10 minutes.

Sandwich the cooled cookies together with raspberry jelly. Using a small piping bag, fill with jelly, and top up the cut-out centers with jelly. Decorate the cookies with confectioners' sugar. Store filled cookies for up to 2 days and unfilled cookies for up to a week.

Makes 1½ dozen

snicker doodles

see variations page 46

Snicker doodles are delicate cookies — but pile your plate high, as one is never enough.

1¼ cups all-purpose flour	¼ tsp. salt
1 tsp. cream of tartar	1 cup (2 sticks) sweet butter
½ tsp. baking soda	¾ cup plus 2 tbsp. superfine sugar
1 tsp. ground cinnamon	1 egg

Preheat the oven to 400°F (200°C). Sift the flour, cream of tartar, baking soda, and half the cinnamon together in a bowl, then add the salt. In a separate bowl, beat the butter and sugar (less 2 tablespoons) together. Add the egg.

Combine the dry ingredients with the butter mixture and mix to a smooth paste. Wrap the dough in parchment and refrigerate for about 30 minutes, or until firm. Mix together the remaining sugar and the cinnamon. Shape the dough into small balls and roll in the cinnamon sugar.

Place the balls at least 2 in. (5 cm.) apart, as the mixture spreads to produce a thin cookie. Flatten each cookie slightly with a fork. Bake for 10 to 12 minutes. Cool for 5 minutes.

Store in an airtight container for up to 5 days.

Makes 2 dozen

beacon hill cookies

see variations page 47

Chocolate lover? Try these light and sticky, ultra-chocolately cookies.

5 oz. bittersweet chocolate
2 egg whites
⅛ tsp. cream of tartar

¼ cup superfine sugar
¾ cup (3½ oz.) chopped pecans
½ tsp. vanilla extract

Preheat the oven to 350°F (175°C).

Melt the chocolate. Beat the egg whites with the cream of tartar until soft peaks form.
Add one third of the sugar, beat for a further minute, then add one third more of the sugar.
Beat until the whites are stiff, and fold in the remaining sugar.

Fold the nuts, chocolate, and vanilla into the mixture.

Drop level teaspoonfuls of the mixture onto parchment-lined baking sheets 1½ in.
(4 cm.) apart. Bake for 10 to 12 minutes until the cookies are cracked and firm to touch.
Lift the parchment sheets onto wire racks and allow the cookies to cool.

Store in an airtight container for up to 3 days.

Makes 2½ dozen

neiman marcus cookies

see variations page 48

The rumor that gave this cookie its rise to fame tells of a customer who inadvertently paid $250 US for this cookie recipe, thinking she was being charged $2.50 US.

½ cup (1 stick) sweet butter
1 cup light brown sugar
1 egg
2 tsp. vanilla extract
1½ cups all-purpose flour

½ tsp. baking soda
½ tsp. baking powder
¼ tsp. salt
1½ tsp. instant coffee powder
1½ cups (8 oz.) semisweet chocolate chips

Preheat the oven to 375°F (190°C).

Beat the butter and sugar together, and add the egg and vanilla.

Sift together the remaining dry ingredients, including the coffee powder. Stir the dry ingredients into the butter mixture and mix in chocolate chips.

Roll into balls. Use your fingers to flatten onto a non-stick baking sheet 2 in. (5 cm.) apart. Bake for 8 to 10 minutes. Cool for 5 minutes.

Store in an airtight container for 4 to 5 days.

Makes 2 dozen

butter cookies

see variations page 49

Simple, rich, and buttery — use only the best quality ingredients for these cookies.

1 cup (2 sticks) sweet butter
¾ cup superfine sugar
1½ tsp. vanilla extract
¼ tsp. salt
2 cups all-purpose flour

Preheat the oven to 350°F (175°C).

Beat the butter, sugar, and vanilla until smooth and creamy, but not fluffy.

Add the salt and flour and mix to a smooth paste.

Shape the dough into a log about 1½ in. (4 cm.) thick, wrap in foil, and refrigerate for 2 hours until the dough is firm. When ready to bake the cookies, cut the log into ¼-in.- (6-mm.-) thick slices. Place the slices 1½ in. (4 cm.) apart on a non-stick baking sheet or use parchment on a standard baking sheet. Bake for 12 to 14 minutes.

Cool on a wire rack and store in an airtight container for up to 5 days.

Makes 2½ dozen

anzac biscuits

see variations page 50

Originally baked annually on April 25th in Australia to commemorate the fallen soldiers at Gallipoli in 1915–1916 during World War I, these cookies are now popular worldwide.

1 cup rolled oats	½ cup (1 stick) sweet butter
1 cup all-purpose flour	2 tbsp. corn syrup
½ cup unrefined light brown sugar	½ tsp. baking soda
½ cup flaked coconut	1 tbsp. hot water

Preheat the oven to 350°F (175°C). Line 2 baking sheets with parchment.

Mix the oats, flour, sugar, and coconut together in a bowl.

Melt the butter and corn syrup in a saucepan over a low heat. Mix the baking soda with the hot water and stir into the butter mixture. Pour the hot butter mixture into the dry ingredients.

Drop tablespoons of the dough onto the sheets 2 in. (5 cm.) apart and flatten slightly with a fork. Bake for 10 to 12 minutes until golden. Cool for 5 minutes.

Store in an airtight container for up to 5 days.

Makes 1½ dozen

tollhouse cookies

see variations page 51

These legendary bars are based on the first American chocolate chip cookie recipe.

2¼ cups all-purpose flour
1 tsp. baking soda
½ tsp. salt
1 cup (2 sticks) sweet butter
¾ cup granulated sugar

¾ cup unrefined light brown sugar
2 tsp. vanilla extract
2 eggs
2 cups (7 oz.) chopped pecans
1 cup (5 oz.) bittersweet chocolate chips

Preheat the oven to 375°F (190°C). Grease and line a 9 x 13-in. (23 x 33-cm.) pan.

Sift together the flour, baking soda, and salt.

Beat the butter and sugars together with the vanilla extract. Beat in the eggs. Stir the flour mixture, nuts and chocolate chips into the mixture.

Spoon the batter into the pan. Bake 25 minutes until golden and firm. Cool in the pan for 5 minutes and cut into squares. Remove from the pan and cool on a wire rack.

Store in an airtight container for 3 to 4 days.

Makes 1 dozen

pretzels

see variations page 52

These are great fun to make, and easy to modify — try dividing up the dough and making different flavored pretzels.

2 cups all-purpose flour
2 tbsp. superfine sugar
2 tsp. active dry yeast
1 cup warm water

¼ cup (½ stick) sweet butter, melted and cooled
½ tsp. salt
1 egg yolk
2 tbsp. granulated sugar

Preheat the oven to 375°F (190°C). Mix 4 tablespoons of the flour with the superfine sugar and dry yeast. Add the warm water and mix to a paste. Put in a warm place for 5 minutes.

Add the yeast mixture and butter to the remaining flour and salt, and mix well. Knead on a floured surface for 5 minutes. Allow the dough to rise in a greased bowl in a warm place for 30 minutes. Divide the dough into 24 pieces. Roll, and form each piece into a pretzel shape.

Place on a greased baking sheet, mix the egg yolk with 1 tablespoon water, and brush the mixture onto the pretzels. Sprinkle with granulated sugar and bake for 10 minutes, or until golden.

Cool on wire racks and store in an airtight container for 2 to 3 days.

Makes 2 dozen

rocky road

see variations page 53

Simple to bake, everyone will love this sweet and sticky snack.

6 tbsp. (¾ stick) sweet butter
1½ cups (5 oz.) graham cracker crumbs
2 tbsp. superfine sugar

1 cup (3½ oz.) chopped pecans
2 cups miniature marshmallows
1 cup (5 oz.) semisweet chocolate chips

Preheat the oven to 350°F (175°C).

Melt the butter and add the graham cracker crumbs and sugar. Press into the base of an 8-in. (20-cm.) square pan lined with foil.

Sprinkle the pecans over the crust, and bake 10 minutes. Leaving the oven on, remove the bars from the oven, and scatter the marshmallows and chocolate chips over the crust.

Return the pan to the oven for about 10 minutes until the marshmallow melts. Cool completely before removing from the pan and cutting into squares.

Store in an airtight container for 3 to 4 days.

Makes 1½ dozen

variations

scottish shortbread

see base recipe page 19

orange shortbread
Prepare the basic shortbread dough, but reduce the vanilla extract to
1 teaspoon and add the zest of 1 orange (2 to 3 teaspoons).

cinnamon shortbread
Prepare the basic shortbread dough, but reduce the vanilla extract to
1 teaspoon and add 1 teaspoon ground cinnamon.

hazelnut shortbread
Prepare the basic shortbread dough, reducing the flour to 1¼ cups and
adding ¼ cup (1 oz.) toasted finely ground hazelnuts.

chocolate-dipped shortbread fingers
Prepare the basic shortbread dough and bake, but omit sprinkling the sugar
after baking. Cut the shortbread into fingers and half-dip each finger into
melted bittersweet chocolate. Remove excess chocolate from the base of
each piece and place the shortbread fingers onto parchment until the
chocolate sets. Store as for ordinary shortbread.

variations

almond biscotti

see base recipe page 20

lemon & pistachio biscotti
Prepare the basic biscotti dough, substituting the grated zest of 1 lemon (2 to 3 teaspoons) for the vanilla extract, and pistachios for the almonds.

chocolate chip & raisin biscotti
Prepare the basic biscotti dough, substituting ½ cup (3 oz.) raisins and ½ cup (3 oz.) semisweet chocolate chips for the almonds.

fig & fennel biscotti
Prepare the basic biscotti dough, substituting ½ cup (3 oz.) chopped dried figs for half the almonds, and 2 teaspoons fennel seeds for the vanilla extract.

variations

peanut butter cookies

see base recipe page 23

peanut butter & chocolate chip cookies
Prepare the basic cookie dough and add ½ cup (3 oz.) bittersweet
chocolate chips.

cream cheese topped peanut butter cookies
Prepare and bake the basic cookie dough. When cool, mix 1 cup (9 oz.)
cream cheese with 2 tablespoons confectioners' sugar, and spread the
cookies with the cream cheese topping. Sprinkle with a few semisweet
chocolate chips. The cookies are best eaten the same day. If not, refrigerate
and eat the next day.

variations

ginger nuts

see base recipe page 24

light ginger nuts
Prepare the basic cookie dough, substituting corn syrup for the molasses. Add 2 tablespoons (1 oz.) chopped candied ginger.

ginger & walnut cookies
Prepare the basic cookie dough and add ½ cup (2 oz.) chopped walnuts.

pineapple & ginger cookies
Prepare the basic cookie dough and add ½ cup (3 oz.) chopped candied pineapple.

ginger, rum, & coconut cookies
Prepare the basic cookie dough and add 2 tablespoons dark rum and substitute ¼ cup flaked coconut for ¼ cup of the all-purpose flour.

variations

linzer cookies

see base recipe page 27

lemon linzer cookies
Prepare the basic cookie dough, double the grated lemon zest (4 to
6 teaspoons) and when baked, fill the cookies with lemon curd. Dust
with confectioners' sugar.

apple linzer cookies
Prepare the basic cookie recipe and when baked, sandwich the cookies
together with apple fruit spread instead of raspberry jelly. Dust with
confectioners' sugar.

almond linzer cookies
Prepare the basic cookie dough, substituting almonds for the hazelnuts. Use
raspberry jelly to fill the cookies and then dust with confectioners' sugar.

variations

snicker doodles

see base recipe page 28

raisin snicker doodles
Prepare the basic cookie dough and add ½ cup (3 oz.) raisins.

chocolate & vanilla snicker doodles
Prepare the basic cookie dough and add 2 teaspoons vanilla extract and ½ cup (3 oz.) bittersweet chocolate chips.

ginger snicker doodles
Prepare the basic cookie dough and add 3 tablespoons (1½ oz.) chopped candied ginger.

variations

beacon hill cookies

see base recipe page 31

spiced beacon hill cookies
Prepare the basic cookie dough and add 1 teaspoon ground cinnamon.

double chocolate beacon hill cookies
Prepare the basic cookie dough and add ½ cup (3 oz.) white chocolate chips.

cherry & walnut beacon hill cookies
Prepare the basic cookie dough and add ½ cup (3 oz.) dried cherries.
Substitute walnuts for the pecans.

variations

neiman marcus cookies

see base recipe page 32

neiman marcus crunch cookies
Prepare the basic cookie dough and add ½ cup (2 oz.) crushed hard
toffee bars.

neiman marcus berry cookies
Prepare the basic cookie dough, omitting the coffee and add ¼ cup (3 oz.)
dried blueberries and ¼ cup (3 oz.) dried cranberries.

neiman marcus ultra chocolate cookies
Prepare the basic cookie dough, substituting Dutch process cocoa powder
for the coffee and adding ½ cup (3 oz.) bittersweet chocolate chips and
½ cup (3 oz.) white chocolate chips.

variations

butter cookies

see base recipe page 34

butter almond cookies
Prepare the basic cookie dough and substitute almond extract for the vanilla extract.

lemon & cinnamon butter cookies
Prepare the basic cookie dough, but reduce the vanilla extract by half and add the grated zest of 1 lemon (2 to 3 teaspoons) and 1 teaspoon ground cinnamon.

ginger butter cookies
Prepare the basic cookie dough, but reduce the vanilla extract by half and add 1 teaspoon ground ginger to the flour, then 3 tablespoons (1½ oz.) chopped candied ginger after the flour is added.

variations

anzac biscuits

see base recipe page 35

macadamia anzac biscuits
Prepare the basic cookie dough, but reduce the coconut by half, and add
¼ cup (1½ oz.) chopped macadamia nuts.

cherry anzac biscuits
Prepare the basic cookie dough and add ¼ cup (2 oz.) chopped red
candied cherries.

chocolate chip anzac biscuits
Prepare the basic cookie dough and add ½ cup (3 oz.) semisweet
chocolate chips.

variations

tollhouse cookies

see base recipe page 37

orange, chocolate, & walnut tollhouse cookies
Prepare the basic cookie dough and add the grated zest of 1 orange (2 to
3 teaspoons). Substitute 3 tablespoons cocoa powder for an equal quantity
of flour, and walnuts for the pecans.

white chocolate & hazelnut tollhouse cookies
Prepare the basic cookie dough, but substitute hazelnuts for the pecans and
white chocolate chips for bittersweet chocolate chips.

mocha tollhouse cookies
Prepare the basic cookie dough, substituting 3 tablespoons cocoa powder for
an equal quantity of flour, and add 1 tablespoon instant powdered coffee.

variations

pretzels

see base recipe page 38

caraway & orange pretzels
Prepare the basic pretzel dough, and after allowing it to rise, add 2 teaspoons caraway seeds and 2 tablespoons (1 oz.) chopped candied orange.

chocolate chip pretzels
Prepare the basic pretzel dough, and after allowing it to rise, add ½ cup (3 oz.) bittersweet chocolate chips.

spiced pretzels
Prepare the basic pretzel dough, and add 1 teaspoon allspice and 1 teaspoon ground ginger.

variations

rocky road

see base recipe page 40

cherry rocky road
Prepare the basic cookie dough and add 1 cup (5 oz.) candied red cherries before adding the marshmallows.

pink rocky road
Prepare the basic cookie dough, but substitute white chocolate chips for the semisweet chocolate chips, add ½ cup (3 oz.) dried cherries, and add pink marshmallows.

caramel fudge rocky road
Prepare and bake the crust. Drizzle crust with 4 tablespoons caramel sauce and ½ cup (3 oz.) chopped fudge pieces before topping with chocolate chips and marshmallows.

peanut rocky road
Prepare the crust and substitute chopped peanuts for the pecans. When the crust is baked, spoon ½ cup (4 oz.) peanut butter over the crust before topping with chocolate chips and marshmallows.

teatime cookies

Cookies were made for eating at teatime — whether with a glass of milk or a mid-afternoon cup of tea. This chapter is full of traditional teatime cookies, from lemon fingers to Viennese pockets; and from ginger crumble cookies to hazelnut chewies.

ginger crumble cookies

see variations page 78

Crisp on the outside and chewy in the middle, these little cookies are packed with spice.

for the cookies

¼ cup (½ stick) sweet butter, melted and cooled
2 tbsp. molasses
½ cup dark brown sugar
1 egg
1 cup all-purpose flour
1 tsp. baking soda
1 tsp. ground ginger
½ tsp. ground cinnamon

¼ tsp. ground allspice
2 tbsp. (1 oz.) finely chopped candied ginger

for the crumble topping

3 tbsp. (⅓ stick) unsalted butter
5 tbsp. all-purpose flour
3 tbsp. rolled oats
3 tbsp. packed light brown sugar

Preheat the oven to 350°F (175°C). Mix the cooled melted butter, molasses, sugar, and egg in a large bowl. Sift the remaining dry ingredients together and stir into the butter mixture. Add the candied ginger. In a separate bowl, combine all the ingredients for the topping.

Roll the cookie dough into balls, using 1½ tablespoons of dough at a time. Place the balls 2 in. (5 cm.) apart on a non-stick baking sheet. Lightly press the cookies into 1¼-in. (3-cm.) rounds and press 1 to 2 teaspoons of the topping onto the dough. Refrigerate the cookies for 1 hour before baking. Bake for 10 to 12 minutes — the cookies will puff up then settle down when baked. Cool on a wire rack. Store in an airtight container for 3 to 4 days.

Makes 1½ dozen

lemon finger cookies

see variations page 79

Serve these elegant, pale lemon fingers with a scented cup of Earl Grey tea.

for the cookies

1 cup (2 sticks) sweet butter
½ cup confectioners' sugar
½ tsp. vanilla extract
Grated zest of 3 lemons (6 to 9 tsp.)
1½ cups all-purpose flour
3 tbsp. cornstarch

for the filling

4 tbsp. (½ stick) sweet butter
1 cup confectioners' sugar
Grated zest of 2 lemons (4 to 6 tsp.)
Juice of ½ lemon (2 tsp.)

Preheat the oven to 350°F (175°C). Beat the butter, confectioners' sugar, vanilla extract, and lemon zest together until light and fluffy. Sift the flour and cornstarch together and stir into the creamed mixture. Using a ½-in. (1-cm.) fluted nozzle and piping bag, pipe the mixture into 2-in. (5-cm.) fingers arranged 1½ in. (4 cm) apart on a non-stick baking sheet. Bake the cookies for 12 minutes. Allow them to firm up before transferring them to a wire rack to cool.

To make the filling, beat the butter and confectioners' sugar with the lemon zest and juice until light and fluffy. Spread the filling onto the flat side of one cookie, then put another cookie on top, and sandwich together.

Store unfilled for 4 to 5 days, filled for 2 to 3 days.

Makes 8 filled cookies

turnover cookies

see variations page 80

Delicate half-moon pastry on the outside, rich and indulgent filling on the inside.

for the cookies

2¼ cups all-purpose flour
¾ cup self-rising flour
¼ cup shortening
¾ cup (1½ stick) sweet butter, diced
¼ cup superfine sugar
2 egg yolks

for the filling

1¾ cups (15¾ oz.) cream cheese
1½ tsp. ground cinnamon
1 cup (5 oz.) raisins

1 egg white
4 tbsp. granulated sugar

Preheat the oven to 375°F (190°C). Grease 2 baking sheets. Sift the flours and cut in the fats until the mixture resembles fine breadcrumbs. Add half the sugar. Mix in egg yolks and 1 to 2 tablespoons of water. Mix to a smooth dough. Wrap in parchment and refrigerate for 20 minutes.

Mix the cream cheese with the remaining sugar, cinnamon, and raisins. Roll out the pastry to ¼ in. (6 mm.) thick and cut out rounds using a 2-in. (5-cm.) cutter. Fill each pastry round with a small amount of filling. Dampen the edges with water and fold in half to give a half-moon shape. Brush with egg white, sprinkle with granulated sugar, and bake 10 to 12 minutes.

Cool on a wire rack. Best eaten fresh. Store leftovers in the refrigerator for 1 to 2 days.

Makes 2 dozen

jelly drops

see variations page 81

These jelly drops are simple to make, and perfect with a cup of herbal tea and a good book before bed.

½ cup (1 stick) sweet butter
⅔ cup superfine sugar
1 egg

1½ cups all-purpose flour
½ tsp. baking powder
¼ cup jelly, any flavor

Preheat the oven to 350°F (175°C). Line 2 baking sheets with parchment.

Beat the butter and sugar until light and fluffy. Add the egg and beat well.

Sift the flour and baking powder and stir into the butter mixture. Roll the mixture into balls and place them at least 2 in. (5 cm.) apart on the baking sheets.

Press a finger into each ball and fill the hole with a little jelly. Bake for 10 minutes until golden. Add a little more jelly while the cookies are still warm.

Cool on a wire rack. Store in an airtight container for 4 to 5 days.

Makes 2 dozen

viennese pockets

see variations page 82

For a luxurious dessert, drizzle with royal icing and accompany with coffee.

for the filling

¼ cup milk
¾ cup superfine sugar
1 cup (4 oz.) ground toasted hazelnuts
2 tbsp. (¼ stick) sweet butter
2 tbsp. dark rum

for the cookies

2½ cups all-purpose flour, sifted
¾ cup plus 1 tbsp. (1½ stick) sweet butter
Grated zest of 1 lemon (2 to 3 tsp.)
1 egg
1 egg white
2 tbsp. granulated sugar

Line 2 baking sheets with parchment. Heat the milk in a saucepan with ¼ cup of the superfine sugar. Stir until the sugar is dissolved and bring to a boil. Remove from the heat, and stir in the hazelnuts, butter, and half the rum. Leave the nut filling to cool, then refrigerate until firm.

Preheat the oven to 350°F (175°C). Combine the flour with the remaining superfine sugar, and cut in the butter. Add the lemon zest, remaining rum, and egg. Mix the dough to a paste. Wrap in parchment and chill the dough for 30 minutes. Roll out the dough to ⅛ in. (3 mm.) thick and cut into 2-in. (5-cm.) squares. Place 2 teaspoons of cooled nut mixture into the center of each square. Fold each corner into the center, and press to seal. Brush the squares with egg white and sprinkle with granulated sugar. Bake 20 minutes. Remove from the oven onto wire racks. When cool, store in an airtight container for 5 days.

Makes 2 dozen

hazelnut chewies

see variations page 83

These small nutty cookies will add a warm and flavorful taste to your afternoon tea.

1 cup (5 oz.) ground toasted hazelnuts
1 cup confectioners' sugar
4 egg whites
¼ tsp. cream of tartar

Preheat the oven to 375°F (190°C). Line 2 baking sheets with parchment.

Put the hazelnuts and sugar in a saucepan.

Beat the egg whites with the cream of tartar until stiff, and combine with hazelnuts in the saucepan. Place the pan over a moderate heat and cook for 5 to 10 minutes until the mixture starts to come away from the sides of the pan.

Spoon the mixture into rough mounds on the parchment 2 in. (5 cm.) apart. Bake for 10 minutes. Transfer to a wire rack, and cool 10 minutes.

Store in an airtight container for 5 to 6 days.

Makes 2 dozen

polenta crescents

see variations page 84

With a hint of lemon, polenta cookies offer a refreshing change from the often sugary teatime snacks.

½ cup (1 stick) sweet butter
1 cup confectioners' sugar
2 egg yolks
Grated zest 1 lemon (2 to 3 tsp.)

2 tsp. vanilla extract
1 cup all-purpose flour
Pinch of baking powder
¼ cup finely ground polenta

Preheat the oven to 325°F (160°C). Grease 2 baking sheets. Beat the butter and sugar together until light and fluffy. Add egg yolks, lemon zest, and vanilla extract.

In a separate bowl, sift the flour and baking powder together, and mix in the polenta. Add to the butter mixture and mix to a smooth dough.

Roll the dough into ½-in. (1-cm.) thick lengths and cut into 4-in. (10-cm.) pieces. Shape these into crescents and space them 2 in. (5 cm.) apart on the baking sheets. Bake 15 minutes until pale in color. Cool on wire racks.

Store in an airtight container for 5 to 7 days.

Makes 2 dozen

butter sandwich cookies

see variations page 85

Delectable butter cookies with a light creamy filling.

for the cookies

1¼ cups (2½ sticks) sweet butter
¾ cup superfine sugar
1½ tsp. vanilla extract
1 egg
¼ tsp. salt
2 cups all-purpose flour

for the filling

⅔ cup confectioners' sugar, sifted
3 tbsp. (3 oz.) cream cheese
4 tbsp. raspberry preserves
Extra confectioners' sugar, to decorate

Preheat the oven to 350°F (175°C). Beat the butter less 2 tablespoons, the sugar, and vanilla until creamy but not fluffy. Beat in the egg. Add salt and flour and mix to a smooth paste. Shape the dough into a flat round, wrap, and refrigerate for 30 minutes, or until firm.

Roll out the dough on a lightly floured surface ⅛-in. (3-mm.) thick, and cut out 2-in. (5-cm.) rounds. Place the rounds 1 in. (2.5 cm.) apart on a non-stick baking sheet. Bake 12 to 15 minutes. Cool on a wire rack.

Beat the remaining butter and confectioners' sugar until the mixture is pale and soft. Stir in the cream cheese. Spread half the cookies with preserves, and half with cream cheese icing. Sandwich and dust with confectioners' sugar. Store in an airtight container for 5 to 7 days.

Makes 1½ dozen

white chocolate & orange cookies

see variations page 86

Delicate chocolate and aromatic orange makes this an elegant accompaniment to a late afternoon cup of tea.

½ cup (1 stick) sweet butter
1 cup superfine sugar
1 egg
Grated zest of 1 orange (2 to 3 tsp.)
1 tsp. vanilla extract

1½ cups all-purpose flour
½ tsp. baking soda
¼ tsp. baking powder
¼ tsp. salt
1½ cups (8 oz.) white chocolate chips

Preheat the oven to 375°F (190°C). Beat the butter and sugar. Add the egg, orange zest, and vanilla extract.

Sift together the dry ingredients. Stir the dry ingredients and chocolate chips into the butter mixture, and combine.

Roll into balls. Use your fingers to flatten onto a non-stick baking sheet 2 in. (5 cm.) apart. Bake 8 to 10 minutes. Cool for 5 minutes.

When cool, store in an airtight container for up to 4 to 5 days.

Makes 2 dozen

pine nut bites

see variations page 87

Bite-sized with added pine nut crunch, these cookies are the perfect antidote for a mid-afternoon snack craving.

2 scant cups ground almonds
1⅓ cups superfine sugar
3 egg whites
1⅓ cups (7 oz.) pine nuts

Preheat the oven to 400°F (200°C).

Mix together the almonds, sugar, and 2 of the egg whites until the dough is smooth and pliable.

Roll the almond dough into small balls, dip them in the remaining egg white, and then into the pine nuts.

Put the balls onto a parchment-lined baking sheet 1½ in. (4 cm.) apart. Bake 5 to 10 minutes until golden and firm. Transfer to a wire rack and cool.

Store in an airtight container for 4 to 5 days.

Makes 2 dozen

melting moments

see variations page 88

The double filling in these small cookies makes for twice the flavor!

for the cookies

1 cup (2 sticks) softened sweet butter
½ cup confectioners' sugar
½ tsp. vanilla extract
1½ cups all-purpose flour
3 tbsp. cornstarch

for the filling

4 tbsp. (½ stick) sweet butter
1 cup confectioners' sugar
2 tsp. vanilla extract
3 tbsp. fruit preserve, any flavor

Preheat the oven to 350°F (175°C). Beat the butter, confectioners' sugar, and vanilla extract together until light and fluffy. Sift the flour and cornstarch and stir into the creamed mixture. Using a ⅓-in. (1-cm.) fluted nozzle and piping bag, pipe the mixture into 1-in. (2½-cm.) rosettes 1½ in. (4 cm.) apart on a non-stick baking sheet.

Bake for 10 to 12 minutes until golden. Allow cookies to firm up slightly before transferring them to a wire rack to cool.

Beat the butter and confectioners' sugar together with the vanilla extract until light and fluffy. Spread fruit preserve onto the bottom of half the cookies and then spread or pipe the filling onto the other halves. Sandwich together. Store in an airtight container for 3 to 4 days.

Makes 1½ dozen

jelly coconut squares

see variations page 89

This coconut and jelly combination makes these treats especially moist and chewy.

½ cup (1 stick) sweet butter
½ cup superfine sugar
1 cup all-purpose flour, sifted
½ tsp. baking powder
1 egg yolk

½ cup jelly
2 eggs
1 tbsp. cornstarch
1 cup flaked coconut
1 cup coconut cream

Preheat the oven to 350°F (175°C). Combine the butter, half of the sugar, flour, and baking powder in a food processor for 1 to 2 minutes. Add the egg yolk.

Process until the mixture forms a smooth dough. Cut a piece of parchment to line an 8 x 10-in. (20 x 30-cm.) pan. Roll out the dough on the parchment and then lift into the pan. Prick with a fork before refrigerating for 10 minutes to set. Bake 12 to 15 minutes until golden. Remove from oven, but keep oven on.

Spread with your favorite jelly. Beat the remaining sugar, eggs, and cornstarch together. Add the flaked coconut and coconut cream and pour over the jelly. Bake for another 15 minutes until firm to touch. Broil tops on high heat for 3 to 4 minutes until golden.

When cool, cut into squares. Store in an airtight container for 3 to 4 days.

Makes 2 dozen

variations

ginger crumble cookies

see base recipe page 55

ginger walnut crumble cookies
Prepare the basic cookie dough and add ½ cup (2 oz.) chopped walnuts.

maple ginger cookies
Prepare the basic cookie dough, substituting maple syrup for the molasses.
Serve without crumble topping.

maple apple crumble cookies
Prepare the basic cookie dough, substituting maple syrup for the molasses.
Increase the cinnamon to 1½ teaspoons and replace the candied ginger
with 4 tablespoons (2 oz.) chopped dried apple pieces.

variations

lemon finger cookies

see base recipe page 56

lemon & chocolate finger cookies
Prepare the basic cookie recipe and assemble the filled cookies in the same way. Half-dip the fingers (on a diagonal) into melted bittersweet chocolate. Place on parchment until the chocolate sets.

spiced lemon finger cookies
Prepare the basic cookie dough, adding ½ teaspoon ground cinnamon to the flour.

lemon & cream cheese filled cookie fingers
Prepare the basic cookie dough. Beat ¾ cup (6¾ oz.) cream cheese and 1 tablespoon confectioners' sugar together and stir in the grated zest of 1 lemon (2 to 3 teaspoons) and 3 tablespoons lemon curd. Sandwich the cookie fingers with the filling.

variations

turnover cookies

see base recipe page 59

cream cheese & jelly turnovers
Prepare the basic cookie dough, omitting the raisins from the cream cheese filling. When filling the turnovers, add ½ teaspoon jelly or fruit preserve to the cream cheese.

apple turnovers
Prepare the basic cookie dough, adding 1 teaspoon ground cinnamon and grated zest of 1 lemon (2 to 3 teaspoons) to the flour. Mix ¼ cup apple butter and raisins and fill the turnovers.

blueberry turnovers
Prepare the basic cookie dough and substitute blueberries for the raisins.

lemon curd turnovers
Prepare the basic cookie recipe and fill the turnovers with lemon curd instead of cream cheese.

variations

jelly drops

see base recipe page 60

lemon curd drops
Prepare the basic cookie dough and substitute lemon curd for the jelly.

apple & cinnamon drops
Prepare the basic cookie dough and add ½ teaspoon ground cinnamon
to the flour. Fill the drops with apple butter or fruit spread instead of jelly.

chocolate drops
Prepare the basic cookie dough, substituting 2 tablespoons Dutch
process cocoa powder for an equal quantity of the flour. Fill each drop
with chocolate-hazelnut spread instead of jelly.

raisin jelly drops
Prepare the basic cookie dough, adding ½ cup (3 oz.) raisins to the dough.

variations

viennese pockets

see base recipe page 63

viennese pockets with pecans & chocolate chips
Prepare the basic cookie recipe, substituting pecans for the hazelnuts and adding ½ cup (3 oz.) bittersweet chocolate chips to the filling.

viennese pockets with cream cheese & poppy seeds
Prepare the basic cookie recipe. Mix ½ cup (4½ oz.) cream cheese with 1 tablespoon poppy seeds and 2 tablespoons bread crumbs. Use to fill the squares.

viennese pockets with apple
Prepare the basic cookie recipe. Peel and finely chop 2 apples and mix with 1 teaspoon ground cinnamon and 2 tablespoons (1 oz.) raisins. Use to fill the squares.

viennese pockets with chocolate & cherries
Prepare the basic cookie recipe, substituting ⅓ cup (2 oz.) chopped candied red cherries for half the hazelnuts and adding ½ cup (3 oz.) bittersweet chocolate chips to the filling.

variations

hazelnut chewies

see base recipe page 64

hazelnut & apricot chewies
Prepare the basic cookie dough. Fold in ½ cup (3 oz.) chopped dried apricots to the mixture before it is baked.

brazil nut & chocolate chip chewies
Prepare the basic cookie dough, substituting brazil nuts for the hazelnuts. Fold in ½ cup (3 oz.) bittersweet chocolate chips to the mixture before it is baked.

almond & cranberry chewies
Prepare the basic cookie dough, substituting almonds for the hazelnuts. Fold in ½ cup (3 oz.) dried cranberries to the mixture before it is baked.

macadamia & pineapple chewies
Prepare the basic cookie dough, substituting macadamias for the hazelnuts. Fold in ½ cup (3 oz.) chopped dried pineapple to the mixture before it is baked.

variations

polenta crescents

see base recipe page 67

chocolate-dipped polenta crescents
When the baked cookies have cooled, half-dip them in melted bittersweet chocolate. Remove excess chocolate and lay them on parchment until the chocolate sets.

oatmeal crescents
Prepare the basic cookie dough, substituting oatmeal for the polenta and 1 teaspoon ground cinnamon for the lemon zest.

orange & chocolate chip crescents
Prepare the basic cookie dough, substituting orange zest for the lemon zest and adding ½ cup (3 oz.) bittersweet chocolate chips.

nut crescents with chocolate-hazelnut filling
Prepare the basic cookie dough, substituting ground hazelnuts for the polenta. Bake and cool the cookies. Spread half the cookie bases with chocolate-hazelnut spread, and sandwich together with the remaining halves.

variations

butter sandwich cookies

see base recipe page 68

orange butter cookies
Prepare the basic cookie dough and add the grated zest of 1 orange
(2 to 3 teaspoons). Prepare the filling and add the grated zest of 1 orange
(2 to 3 teaspoons). Fill and sandwich the cookies.

maple butter cookies with pecan filling
Prepare the basic cookie dough and substitute maple syrup for half of
the sugar. Prepare the filling and add 2 tablespoons bourbon and ¼ cup
(1 oz.) chopped pecans. Fill and sandwich the cookies.

spiced butter cookies
Prepare the basic cookie dough and add 1 teaspoon ground cinnamon.
Prepare the filling, and sandwich together.

variations

white chocolate & orange cookies

see base recipe page 71

white chocolate & peanut butter cookies
Prepare the basic cookie dough, omitting the orange zest and adding
¼ cup (2 oz.) smooth peanut butter.

dark chocolate & orange cookies
Prepare the basic cookie dough and use bittersweet chocolate chips
instead of the white chocolate chips.

white chocolate, orange, & cranberry cookies
Prepare the basic cookie dough, adding ½ cup (3 oz.) dried cranberries.

variations

pine nut bites

see base recipe page 72

lemon & pine nut bites
Prepare the basic cookie dough and add the grated zest of 1 lemon
(2 to 3 teaspoons).

chocolate chip pine nut bites
Prepare the basic cookie dough and add ½ cup (3 oz.) bittersweet
chocolate chips.

cherry & walnut bites
Prepare the basic cookie dough and add ½ cup (2 oz.) chopped candied
red cherries to the almond mixture. Substitute chopped walnuts for the
pine nuts.

variations

melting moments

see base recipe page 75

malted milk melting moments
Prepare the basic cookie dough, substituting 2 tablespoons
malted milk powder for 2 tablespoons of the flour in the cookie
recipe and 2 tablespoons malted milk powder for 2 tablespoons of
the confectioners' sugar in the filling. Omit the fruit preserves.

mocha melting moments
Prepare the basic cookie dough, substituting 2 teaspoons instant coffee
powder for the vanilla extract, and 2 tablespoons cooled melted bittersweet
chocolate for the vanilla extract in the filling. Omit the fruit preserves.

ginger melting moments
Prepare the basic cookie dough, substituting 1 teaspoon ground ginger
for the vanilla extract in the cookie recipe, and adding 2 tablespoons (1 oz.)
chopped candied ginger in the filling. Omit the fruit preserves.

variations

jelly coconut squares

see base recipe page 76

coconut & chocolate squares
Prepare the basic cookie dough and substitute chocolate-hazelnut
spread for the jelly. Add ½ cup (3 oz.) semisweet chocolate chips to
the coconut topping.

pineapple & coconut squares
Prepare the basic cookie dough, and use pineapple jelly. Add ½ cup (2 oz.)
chopped candied pineapple to the coconut topping.

rum & coconut squares
Prepare the basic cookie dough and add 2 tablespoons dark rum to the
coconut topping.

caramel fudge coconut squares
Prepare the basic cookie dough and use caramel spread instead of jelly. Add
½ cup (3 oz.) chopped fudge pieces to the coconut topping.

cookies for kids

Kids love cookies — both eating them and making
them. This chapter is full of appealing ideas that
are perfect for both young and old. Encourage
your kids to read with alphabet cookies, make
gingerbread bears together and let them roll out
the dough, or create a traffic jam on the table with
cookie cars!

fruit & nut refrigerator cookies

see variations page 113

These are likely to become a favorite with everyone who tries them.

1 lb. bittersweet chocolate	2 cups (7 oz.) toasted hazelnuts, chopped rough
1 cup (2 sticks) sweet butter	1 cup (5 oz.) raisins
4 cups crumbled graham crackers	1 cup (5 oz.) halved red candied cherries

Line a 9 x 13-in. (23 x 33-cm.) baking sheet with a layer of parchment.

Melt the chocolate and butter together in a large mixing bowl. Add the remaining ingredients. Stir thoroughly to ensure the ingredients are well-mixed.

Spoon mixture onto a lined tray, and level the surface with a palette knife. Cover and refrigerate for 2 to 3 hours or until firm enough to turn out and cut into wedges.

Store in the refrigerator for 5 to 7 days.

Makes 2 dozen

pizza cookie

see variations page 114

A giant-size chewy cookie topped with cream cheese icing and brightly colored candy. This would make a fun surprise for a child's party.

for the cookie
½ cup (1 stick) sweet butter
1 cup superfine sugar
1 egg
1 tsp. vanilla extract
1½ cups all-purpose flour
½ tsp. baking soda

for the topping
½ cup (1 stick) sweet butter
2 cups confectioners' sugar
½ cup (4½ oz.) cream cheese
1 cup (5 oz.) candies
2 tbsp. sugar strands

Preheat the oven to 350°F (175°C) and line a 12-in. (30-cm.) pizza tray or baking sheet with parchment.

Beat the butter and superfine sugar together. Then add the egg and vanilla extract. Sift the flour and baking soda and stir into the batter. Spread the dough onto the pizza tray or baking sheet. Bake for 18 to 20 minutes until golden. Remove from the oven and allow to cool before transferring to a wire rack.

Beat the butter and confectioners' sugar together and then beat in the cream cheese. Spread over the cooled cookie and decorate with candies and sugar strands.

Makes 1 large cookie

ice cream cookies

see variations page 115

For a fun dessert or party treat, pile up a bunch of ice cream cookies on a plate, drizzle with fudge sauce, and then sprinkle with candies.

1 cup all-purpose flour	1 egg
½ tsp. baking soda	1 tsp. vanilla extract
¼ cup (½ stick) sweet butter	2 cups cornflakes or crisped rice cereal
¼ cup vegetable shortening	½ cup melted semisweet chocolate
¾ cup superfine sugar	4 cups vanilla ice cream

Preheat the oven to 350°F (175°C) and lightly grease two baking sheets. Sift the flour and baking soda. Beat the butter and shortening with the sugar until light and fluffy. Add the egg and vanilla extract and stir through the sifted flour and cereal.

Roll the dough into small balls. Place on baking sheets 2 in. (5 cm.) apart and flatten slightly. Bake for 8 to 10 minutes, then leave to cool on wire racks. Once completely cool, brush cookie bases with melted chocolate and put them in the fridge to set for a few minutes. Spoon about ¼ cup ice cream onto each cookie base and sandwich with the other cookie half.

Put ice cream cookies in the freezer to harden and then transfer to an airtight container in the freezer. Best eaten within 4 days.

Makes 1 dozen

peanut butter jelly thumbprints

see variations page 116

With a thumbful of jelly, these peanut butter delights will leave fingerprints all over the cookie jar.

¾ cup superfine sugar
¼ cup light brown sugar
1 cup (8 oz.) peanut butter

1 egg
½ tsp. vanilla extract
⅓ cup raspberry jelly

Preheat the oven to 375°F (190°C).

Combine all the ingredients in a large bowl, except the jelly. Mix until smooth.

Roll the mixture into 1-in. (2.5-cm.) balls. If they are a bit sticky, use a little flour on your fingers.

Place the balls onto non-stick baking sheets about 2 in. (5 cm.) apart and, using a floured thumb, make a deep impression in each ball of dough. Bake for 10 to 12 minutes. Cool on a wire rack.

Fill each impression with jelly. Store in an airtight container for 4 to 5 days.

Makes 3 dozen

gingerbread bears

see variations page 117

Gingerbread bears are great fun to make and decorate. Try piping names onto them and putting them in party bags for a child's party.

2¾ cups all-purpose flour
1 tsp. baking soda
1 tsp. ground cinnamon
1½ tsp. ground ginger
¼ tsp. ground allspice
½ cup light brown sugar

4 tbsp. molasses
1 egg
⅓ cup (¾ stick) melted sweet butter
Royal icing to decorate
½ cup (2 oz.) candies

Lightly grease 2 baking sheets. Sift the flour, baking soda, and spices together in a bowl. Add the sugar, molasses, egg, and butter and mix to a smooth paste. Chill the dough until firm.

Preheat the oven to 375°F (190°C). Roll out the dough onto a lightly floured surface to ¼ in. (6 mm.) thick. Cut out the gingerbread bears using a floured cookie cutter.

Bake for 8 to 10 minutes. Cool on a wire rack. Decorate with royal icing. Use icing to affix candies.

Store in an airtight container for 7 to 10 days.

Makes 1 dozen

oat delights

see variations page 118

Very simple to make, oat delights are a great idea if the kids want to play chef and bake something on their own.

1 cup rolled oats	2 tbsp. (¼ stick) sweet butter
1 cup flaked coconut	2 tbsp. corn syrup
4 oz. semisweet chocolate, melted	3 tbsp. Dutch process cocoa powder, sifted

Mix the oats and coconut together in a large bowl.

Melt the chocolate and butter, and add the corn syrup. Pour the oats and coconut into the melted chocolate mixture and stir to combine.

Add the Dutch process cocoa powder and stir to incorporate. Roll the mixture into balls. If the mixture is too sticky, add a little more cocoa powder.

Refrigerate the balls on parchment-lined baking sheets. When they are firm, transfer to an airtight container in the refrigerator for 5 to 7 days.

Makes 1½ dozen

carnival bars

see variations page 119

For carnivals, birthdays, or any other celebration, these bars are easy to package, pretty to serve, and delicious to eat.

⅓ cup (⅔ stick) sweet butter
½ cup light brown sugar
1 egg
1 tsp. vanilla extract

1¼ cups all-purpose flour
½ tsp. baking powder
½ cup (3½ oz.) candies

Preheat the oven to 350°F (175°C). Line a 9-in. (23-cm.) square pan with parchment.

Beat the butter and sugar and then add the egg and vanilla.

Sift the flour and baking powder and beat into the mixture. Stir in the candies.

Press the mixture into the pan and bake for 20 to 25 minutes until golden brown. Cool in the pan and then cut into squares.

Store in an airtight container for 5 to 7 days.

Makes 2 dozen

coconut & cherry macaroons

see variations page 120

These sweet treats are so addictive, it will be hard to stop at one.

2 cups shredded or flaked coconut
4 egg whites
¾ cup superfine sugar

2 tsp. vanilla extract
Pinch of salt
½ cup (3 oz.) chopped red candied cherries

Preheat the oven to 350°F (175°C). Line 2 baking sheets with parchment.

Combine all the ingredients except the cherries in a large heat-proof bowl over a pan of simmering water. Stir the mixture constantly for 6 minutes, or until the egg whites have started to thicken. The mixture is ready when its consistency is homogenous and holds shape.

Remove bowl from pan and stir in the cherries. Drop large spoonfuls of the mixture about 2 in. (5 cm.) apart on the lined sheets. Bake 15 minutes until the macaroons are golden.

Slide the parchment and cookies onto wire racks and allow to cool completely.

Store in an airtight container for 3 to 4 days.

Makes 1½ dozen

blueberry & white chocolate crunchies

see variations page 121

Quick to make, but even quicker to eat, blueberries give these crunchies a tart twist.

1 lb. white chocolate, chopped
¼ cup (½ stick) sweet butter
4 cups puffed rice cereal
1 cup (5 oz.) dried blueberries

Line a 9-in.- (23-cm.-) square pan with parchment.

Melt the chocolate and butter, then stir in the cereal and blueberries.

Spoon the mixture into the pan. Refrigerate until set and then cut into squares.

Store in an airtight container for 5 to 7 days.

Makes 2 dozen

alphabet cookies

see variations page 122

Whet your child's appetite for spelling . . . cookie-style!

¾ cup (1½ sticks) sweet butter
1 cup superfine sugar
1½ tsp. vanilla extract
2½ cups all-purpose flour, sifted

1 egg
1 egg yolk
Royal icing, to decorate

Line 2 baking sheets with parchment. Blend the butter, sugar, and vanilla extract in a food processor until smooth. Add the flour, egg, and egg yolk and process to a smooth dough. Wrap in parchment and refrigerate until firm.

Preheat the oven to 350°F (175°C). Roll out the dough either on a lightly floured work surface or between 2 sheets of parchment to ¼ in. (6 mm.) thick.

Cut out letters using cookie cutters or homemade stencils. Place the cookies on the sheets and bake 10 to 12 minutes. Cool on wire racks.

Store in an airtight container for one week.

Makes 3 dozen

jammie dodgers

see variations page 123

Introducing the jammie dodger: every kid's favorite — every adult's soft spot.

2 cups all-purpose flour
¼ cup superfine sugar
Pinch of salt
¾ cup (1½ sticks) sweet butter

1 tsp. vanilla extract
5 tbsp. raspberry jelly
2 tbsp. confectioners' sugar

Put the flour, sugar, salt, butter, and vanilla extract in a food processor and pulse until the mixture clumps. Work the dough into a flat round. Wrap in parchment and refrigerate until firm.

Preheat the oven to 350°F (175°C). Roll out the dough on a floured surface to ⅛ in. (3 mm.) thick. Cut out rounds using a 1½ in. (4 cm.) cookie cutter. Place half the cookies on parchment-lined baking sheets. Using a smaller round cutter, cut out the centers from the remaining cookies. Bake the cookies on separate baking sheets for 8 to 10 minutes, until golden.

Allow the cookies to cool before sandwiching together with jelly. Make a small parchment piping bag, fill with jelly, and pipe more jelly into the cut-out centers. Dust the cookies with confectioners' sugar. Store unfilled cookies in an airtight container for a week, and filled cookies for 3 days.

Makes 1½ dozen

cookie cars

see variations page 124

You can make the cookies, but let them design the cars. This recipe is a great project for a rainy afternoon, but be forewarned, there will be traffic jams on the table in no time.

1¼ cups all-purpose flour
¼ tsp. baking powder
Pinch of salt
½ cup (1 stick) sweet butter
¾ cup superfine sugar

1 tbsp. milk
1 tsp. vanilla extract
Royal icing, food color, and candies or silver
    balls to decorate

Sift the flour and baking powder, then add the salt. In a separate bowl, beat the butter and sugar until pale and fluffy, then beat in the egg, milk, and vanilla extract.

Gradually add the flour mixture and mix to a smooth dough. Wrap in parchment and refrigerate until firm.

Preheat the oven to 400°F (200°C). Roll out the dough onto a lightly floured surface or between 2 sheets of parchment. Using a floured cutter, cut shapes from the dough. Place on non-stick baking sheets and bake 8 to 10 minutes. Cool completely on wire racks. Decorate with royal icing.

Store in an airtight container for 4 to 5 days.

Makes 2 dozen

pecan chocolate mallow bars

see variations page 125

Crunchy, sticky chocolate bars to get your fingers and teeth stuck into. A great recipe to make with the kids — you do the melting, and let them throw on the marshmallows.

3 oz. bittersweet chocolate
½ cup (1 stick) sweet butter
1 cup light brown sugar
2 eggs

½ cup all-purpose flour, sifted
1 tsp. vanilla extract
1 cup (3½ oz.) chopped pecans
3 cups large pink and white marshmallows

Preheat the oven to 350°F (175°C). Grease and line a 9-in.- (23-cm.-) square pan.

Melt the chocolate. Beat the butter and sugar until light and fluffy, then beat in the eggs. Stir in the flour. Then stir in the melted chocolate, butter, vanilla, and pecans.

Pour the mixture into the pan. Bake for 20 minutes, remove from the oven and cover with marshmallows. Return to the oven for 5 to 10 minutes until the marshmallows have melted.

Allow to cool in the pan and then refrigerate until completely cold before cutting into bars.

Store in an airtight container for 5 to 7 days.

Makes 2 dozen

variations

fruit & nut refrigerator cookies

see base recipe page 91

fudge pecan refrigerator cookies
Prepare the basic cookie dough, substituting 2 cups (7 oz.) toasted chopped pecans for the hazelnuts, and 1 cup (5 oz.) chopped fudge for the candied cherries.

ginger crunch refrigerator cookies
Prepare the basic cookie dough, using ginger snaps instead of graham crackers, and 3 tablespoons (1½ oz.) chopped candied ginger instead of the candied cherries.

totally nuts refrigerator cookies
Prepare the basic cookie dough, using 1 cup (3½ oz.) toasted chopped pecans instead of the raisins and cherries, and stir in 4 tablespoons (2 oz.) smooth peanut butter.

variations

pizza cookie

see base recipe page 92

ice cream pizza cookie
Prepare the basic cookie pizza. When the cookie has cooled, spread with
6 tablespoons chocolate-hazelnut spread. Top with scoops of vanilla,
chocolate, and strawberry ice cream and drizzle with chocolate sauce.
Serve immediately.

marshmallow pizza cookie
Prepare the basic cookie pizza. When the cookie has cooled, spread with
peanut butter and jelly. Top with handfuls of mini marshmallows.

tutti frutti pizza cookie
Prepare the basic cookie pizza. When the cookie has cooled, spread with
whipped cream. Top with fresh fruits including strawberries, sliced bananas,
and blueberries.

variations

ice cream cookies

see base recipe page 95

mint-chocolate ice cream cookies
Prepare the basic cookie dough. Substitute 2 tablespoons Dutch process cocoa powder for an equal amount of the flour. Add ¼ cup (2 oz.) crushed mint candies. Fill the cookies with mint-chocolate ice cream.

nutty ice cream cookies
Prepare the basic cookie dough, then add 2 tablespoons (1 oz.) smooth peanut butter and ½ cup (2 oz.) chopped pecans to the cookie mixture. Fill the cookies with caramel nut ice cream.

lemon & raspberry ice cream cookies
Prepare the basic cookie dough and add the grated zest of 2 lemons (4 to 6 teaspoons). Substitute white chocolate for the melted semisweet chocolate, and fill the cookies with raspberry or berry swirl ice cream.

variations

peanut butter jelly thumbprints

see base recipe page 96

peanut butter chocolate chip & jelly thumbprints
Prepare the basic cookie dough and add ½ cup (3 oz.) bittersweet
chocolate chips to the dough.

peanut butter & chocolate thumbprints
Prepare the basic cookie dough and add ½ cup (3 oz.) bittersweet
chocolate chips to the dough. Fill the thumbprint impressions with
chocolate-hazelnut spread.

peanut butter & cranberry thumbprints
Prepare the basic cookie dough, then add ½ cup (3 oz.) dried cranberries
and fill the thumbprint impressions with cranberry jelly.

variations

gingerbread bears

see base recipe page 99

raisin gingerbread bears
Prepare the basic cookie dough and add ½ cup (3 oz.) raisins. Bake
and decorate.

extra ginger gingerbread bears
Prepare the basic cookie dough and add 4 tablespoons (2 oz.) chopped
candied ginger. Bake and decorate.

crunchy gingerbread bears
Prepare the basic cookie dough, then brush the cut-out gingerbread men
with egg white and sprinkle with raw brown sugar. Bake and decorate.

variations

oat delights

see base recipe page 100

cherry & oat delights
Prepare the basic cookie dough, adding 1 cup (5 oz.) chopped candied red cherries.

walnut oat delights
Prepare the basic cookie dough, adding 1 cup (3½ oz.) chopped walnuts.

peanut butter oat delights
Prepare the basic cookie dough, substituting ½ cup (4 oz.) smooth peanut butter for the chocolate.

variations

carnival bars

see base recipe page 101

chocolate mint carnival bars
Prepare the basic cookie dough, substituting 2 tablespoons Dutch process cocoa powder for 2 tablespoons of the flour. Substitute peppermint extract for the vanilla extract, and chocolate chips for the candy.

peanut butter & caramel carnival bars
Prepare the basic cookie dough, adding ½ cup (4 oz.) peanut butter. Use caramel candies.

fruity carnival bars
Prepare the basic cookie dough and substitute ½ cup (3 oz.) chopped red candied cherries and ½ cup (3 oz.) chopped candied pineapple instead of the candies.

coconut & cherry macaroons

see base recipe page 103

chocolate chip macaroons
Prepare the basic cookie dough and substitute semisweet chocolate chips for the cherries.

coconut & pineapple macaroons
Prepare the basic cookie dough and substitute ½ cup (3 oz.) chopped candied pineapple for the cherries.

chocolate dipped macaroons
Prepare the macaroons, and when they are completely cool, half-dip them in tempered bittersweet chocolate.

variations

blueberry & white chocolate crunchies

see base recipe page 104

chocolate nut & raisin crunchies
Prepare the basic cookie dough, substituting semisweet chocolate
for the white chocolate and ½ cup (2 oz.) chopped pecans and ½ cup
(3 oz.) raisins for the dried blueberries.

chocolate & cherry crunchies
Prepare the basic cookie dough, substituting bittersweet chocolate for
the white chocolate and dried cherries for the blueberries.

chocolate mallow & strawberry crunchies
Prepare the basic cookie dough, then add ½ cup miniature marshmallows.
Substitute dried strawberries for the blueberries.

variations

alphabet cookies

see base recipe page 107

candy alphabet cookies
Prepare the basic cookie dough and add 1 cup (5 oz.) crushed candies to the dough after removing it from the food processor and before chilling.

orange alphabet cookies
Prepare the basic cookie dough, adding the grated zest of 1 orange (2 to 3 teaspoons).

double-decker alphabet cookies
Prepare the basic cookie dough and cut out 2 of each letter. Bake and cool the cookies, then sandwich them together with your favorite icing. Dust the cookie tops with confectioners' sugar or decorate with royal icing.

variations

jammie dodgers

see base recipe page 108

jammie dodgers with icing
Prepare the basic cookie recipe and bake. When the cookies have cooled,
spread all of the cookie bases first with vanilla icing and then with fruit
preserve. Sandwich the halves together.

lemon jammie dodgers
Prepare the basic cookie recipe and bake, adding the grated zest of 1 lemon
(2 to 3 teaspoons). When the cookies are cool, spread with lemon curd and
lemon icing, and sandwich the halves together.

maple jammie dodgers
Prepare the basic cookie dough, substituting 1 tablespoon maple syrup for
1 tablespoon of the superfine sugar. When the cookies are cool, fill with
maple icing.

variations

cookie cars

see base recipe page 111

chocolate cookie cars
Prepare the basic cookie dough, substituting 2 tablespoons Dutch process cocoa powder for 2 tablespoons of the flour. Decorate with chocolate icing and candies.

lemon & spice cookie cars
Prepare the basic cookie dough, then add the grated zest of 1 lemon (2 to 3 teaspoons) to the beaten butter and ½ teaspoon ground allspice to the sifted flour.

hazelnut cookie cars
Prepare the basic cookie dough, substituting ¼ cup (1 oz.) ground toasted hazelnuts for ¼ cup flour.

variations

pecan chocolate mallow bars

see base recipe page 112

peanut chocolate mallow bars
Prepare the basic cookie dough and add ¼ cup (2 oz.) smooth
peanut butter to the mix. Substitute peanuts for the pecans.

cherry chocolate mallow bars
Prepare the basic cookie dough and substitute red candied cherries
for the pecans.

orange chocolate walnut mallow bars
Prepare the basic cookie dough, adding the grated zest of 1 orange
(2 to 3 teaspoons) to the mix. Substitute walnuts for the pecans.

chocolate cookies

White chocolate chunk cookies, chocolate shortbread, chocolate pinwheels, chewy chocolate cookies, and cookies that are chocolate-dipped, drizzled, and swirled — this chapter is dunked in ... chocolate, of course.

dalmatian bars

see variations page 147

These nutty chocolate bars are simple to make and, as their name suggests, are "spotted" with chocolate and nuts.

5 oz. bittersweet chocolate
¾ cup (1½ sticks) sweet butter
4 eggs
1¾ cups superfine sugar
2 tsp. vanilla extract

1¼ cups all-purpose flour, sifted
1 tsp. baking powder, sifted
¼ tsp. salt
1 cup (5 oz.) macadamia nuts
1½ cups (8 oz.) white chocolate chips

Preheat the oven to 375°F (190°C). Grease and line a 9 x 13-in. (23 x 33-cm.) pan with parchment.

Melt the chocolate and the butter together. Beat the eggs and sugar with the vanilla and stir into the chocolate mixture. Stir in the dry ingredients, and lastly, stir in the macadamia nuts and three-quarters of the chocolate chips.

Spoon into the prepared pan, level the surface and sprinkle with the remaining chocolate chips. Bake for 20 to 25 minutes or until firm. Cool in the pan and cut into bars.

Store in an airtight container for 4 to 5 days.

Makes 2 dozen

cream cheese & chocolate double deckers

see variations page 148

Crumbly cookies filled with a sweet cream cheese — simply luxurious.

for the cookies

1 cup all-purpose flour, sifted
½ tsp. baking soda
½ cup (4½ oz.) cream cheese
¼ cup (½ stick) sweet butter
¾ cup superfine sugar
1 egg
3½ oz. bittersweet chocolate, melted

for the filling

½ cup (4½ oz.) cream cheese
1 cup confectioners' sugar, sifted

Preheat the oven to 350°F (175°C). Sift the flour and baking soda and set aside. Beat half of the cream cheese and the butter until soft and smooth, then add the sugar and egg, and beat until light and fluffy. Stir in the chocolate and then the flour mixture. Mix to a smooth dough. Drop spoonfuls of dough onto baking sheets, and bake for 10 to 12 minutes until firm at the edges. Remove from the sheets onto wire racks, and allow to cool.

Beat the remaining cream cheese and confectioners' sugar until soft and smooth and spread on the bases of half the cookies. Sandwich with the remaining halves.

When completely cool, store in an airtight container in the fridge for 2 to 3 days.

Makes 2 dozen

white chocolate chunk cookies

see variations page 149

For all those white chocolate fans — this one's for you.

½ cup (1 stick) sweet butter
1 cup superfine sugar
1 egg
2 tsp. vanilla extract
1¼ cups all-purpose flour
½ tsp. baking soda

½ tsp. baking powder
¼ tsp. salt
¼ cup oatmeal
1½ cups (8 oz.) chopped white
    chocolate chunks

Preheat the oven to 375°F (190°C). Beat the butter and sugar and then add the egg and vanilla. Sift together dry ingredients and stir in the oatmeal. Incorporate the mixed dry ingredients and chocolate into the butter mixture.

Roll into balls and use your fingers to flatten onto a non-stick baking sheet 2 in. (5 cm.) apart. Bake for 8 to 10 minutes. Cool 5 minutes.

When cool, store in an airtight container for 4 to 5 days.

Makes 2 dozen

chocolate-drizzled ginger cookies

see variations page 150

Crisp, spicy, and smothered in dark chocolate, this is a more sophisticated cookie.

1 egg
1 egg yolk
1 cup superfine sugar
½ cup (1 stick) sweet butter
2¼ cups all-purpose flour
¼ tsp. baking soda

1½ tsp. ground ginger
¼ tsp. salt

for the topping

6 oz. bittersweet chocolate, melted

Grease 2 baking sheets. Mix together the egg, egg yolk, and sugar and then stir in the melted butter. Sift the flour, baking soda, ginger, and salt into a bowl. Add the dry ingredients to the egg mixture and mix to combine. Chill the dough until firm.

Preheat the oven to 375°F (190°C). Roll the dough out between parchment or plastic to ⅛ in. (3 mm.) thick. Cut out 2-in. (5-cm.) rounds, and lay them on baking sheets. Bake for 15 minutes until golden.

Cool on a wire rack. Dip a fork in the melted chocolate, drizzle chocolate over each cookie, and place on parchment for the chocolate to set. Store in an airtight container for 5 to 7 days.

Makes 2 dozen

marbled chocolate & vanilla cookies

see variations page 151

These attractive little cookies will go perfectly with your afternoon coffee.

2½ cups all-purpose flour
¾ cup confectioners' sugar
1 cup plus 2 tbsp. (2 sticks) sweet butter
2 tbsp. heavy cream

2 tsp. vanilla extract
3 tbsp. Dutch process cocoa powder, sifted
1 egg white
2 tbsp. granulated sugar

Grease 2 baking sheets. Sift the flour and confectioners' sugar together and cut in the butter.

When the mixture starts to come together, add the cream and vanilla extract. Divide the mixture in half and add the cocoa powder to one half. Knead the separate doughs lightly until smooth. Mix small amounts of each dough together and roll into 4 x 1½-in. (4-cm.) wide logs. Wrap in parchment and refrigerate until firm.

Preheat the oven to 375°F (190°C). Brush each log with egg white and roll in granulated sugar. Cut into ¼-in. (6-mm.) thick slices. Place the cookie slices on the baking sheets and bake for 8 to 10 minutes. Cool on a wire rack.

When completely cool, store in an airtight container for 5 to 7 days.

Makes 3½ dozen

chocolate shortbread

see variations page 152

Rich shortbread with a chocolate twist — use this recipe as a base for cheesecakes or other desserts, or enjoy on its own with a large glass of milk.

1½ cup all-purpose flour
6 tbsp. Dutch process cocoa powder
¼ tsp. salt
½ cup superfine sugar

¾ cup (1½ sticks) sweet butter
2 tsp. vanilla extract
2 tsp. granulated sugar

Preheat the oven to 300°F (150°C). Line a 7 x 11-in. (18 x 28-cm.) pan with foil.

Sift the flour and cocoa powder into a large bowl and add the salt. Beat the butter and sugar. Add the vanilla extract and stir in the dry ingredients. Knead the dough until it starts to clump together, and then press into the pan.

Bake for 45 to 50 minutes. The shortbread will look cooked before it actually is, so ensure that it is baked for the full amount of time.

Remove from the oven, sprinkle with granulated sugar, and cut into fingers. Cool 20 minutes before removing from the pan. Store in an airtight container for up to 5 days.

Makes 1½ dozen

chocolate spice cookies

see variations page 153

These full-flavored cookies need to be covered in quality bittersweet chocolate for the best results.

1¼ cups all-purpose flour
2 tbsp. cocoa powder
½ tsp. baking powder
½ tsp. ground allspice
Pinch of salt

¼ cup (½ stick) sweet butter
¾ cup light brown sugar
1 egg
3 tbsp. maple syrup

Line 2 baking sheets with parchment.

Sift the flour, cocoa powder, baking powder, spices, and salt in a bowl. In a separate bowl, beat the butter and sugar until light and fluffy, then beat in the egg. Stir in the maple syrup and then add the dry ingredients. Wrap and refrigerate until firm.

Preheat the oven to 375°F (190°C). Roll out the dough equally between 2 sheets of plastic. Peel off the plastic and cut the dough with a floured 2 in. (5 cm.) cutter. Put the cookies on the baking sheets and chill until firm. Remove from refrigerator and bake for 8 to 10 minutes. Slide the parchment onto wire racks to cool.

When completely cool, store in an airtight container for 5 to 7 days.

Makes 2½ dozen

chocolate & orange sandwich cookies

see variations page 154

Chocolate and orange is a great flavor combination — try these cookies and you'll see why.

for the cookies

8 oz. bittersweet chocolate, chopped coarse
⅓ cup all-purpose flour
¼ tsp. baking powder
Pinch of salt
2 eggs
½ cup superfine sugar
Grated zest of 1 orange (2 to 3 tsp.)

for the filling

6 tbsp. (¾ stick) sweet butter
1 cup confectioners' sugar
Grated zest (2 to 3 tsp.) and juice
    (3 tbsp.) of 1 orange

Preheat the oven to 350°F (175°C). Line 2 baking sheets with parchment. Melt the chocolate and allow it to cool slightly. Sift the flour, baking powder, and salt together in another bowl. Whisk the eggs, sugar, and orange zest, and stir into the melted chocolate. Stir in the flour. Spoon small amounts of the dough onto the baking sheets 2 in. (5 cm.) apart. Bake for 10 to 25 minutes. Slide the parchment onto cooling racks.

Beat the filling ingredients together until fluffy. Spread a bit of orange icing on the base of a cookie, and sandwich with another. Store the cookies in an airtight container for 4 to 5 days.

Makes 1½ dozen

chocolate pinwheels

see variations page 155

Great favorites to both make and eat — and they look so very impressive.

3½ oz. bittersweet chocolate, chopped coarse
2½ cups all-purpose flour
2 tsp. baking powder
¼ tsp. salt

½ cup (1 stick) sweet butter
⅔ cup superfine sugar
2 eggs
2 tsp. vanilla extract

Line 2 baking sheets with parchment. Melt the chocolate and allow it to cool slightly. Sift the flour, baking powder, and salt together in another bowl. In a separate bowl, beat butter and sugar until soft and creamy, then add the eggs and vanilla extract. Stir the dry ingredients into the butter mixture to form a paste. Divide the mix between 2 bowls. Mix chocolate into one half of the dough. Wrap in parchment and refrigerate the doughs until firm.

Roll out the chocolate dough on floured parchment and brush off any excess flour. Roll out the plain dough on another sheet of parchment and lay the plain dough on top of the chocolate dough. Roll lightly with the rolling pin and trim the long edges. Roll up the dough tightly from the longer side. Wrap in parchment and refrigerate until firm.

Preheat the oven to 375°F (190°C). Slice thin and lay on baking sheets. Bake for 8 to 10 minutes. Cool on a wire rack, and store in an airtight container for 5 to 7 days.

Makes 3 dozen

chocolate fingers

see variations page 156

Richly flavored chocolate fingers are a tempting treat for the entire family.

5 oz. semisweet chocolate
½ cup (1 stick) sweet butter
1 cup (9 oz.) cream cheese
¾ cup superfine sugar
1 egg

1 tsp. vanilla extract
2 cups all-purpose flour
½ tsp. baking powder
½ cup (3 oz.) white chocolate chips
½ cup (2 oz.) coarsely chopped toasted pecans

Preheat the oven to 375°F (190°C). Line a 9 x 13-in. (23 x 33-cm.) pan.

Melt the chocolate. Beat the butter, cream cheese, sugar, egg, and vanilla extract until soft and smooth. Sift the flour and baking powder and stir into the butter mixture. Spread the mixture into the pan and level the surface. Bake for 15 to 20 minutes until firm.

Remove from the oven, drizzle the melted chocolate over the top, and sprinkle with the remaining ingredients. Allow to cool and set, and then cut into fingers.

Store in an airtight container for 5 to 7 days.

Makes 2 dozen

chewy chocolate cookies

see variations page 157

Simply irresistible cookies, perfect for any time of day.

6 oz. bittersweet chocolate, chopped
¼ cup (½ stick) sweet butter
⅓ cup all-purpose flour
¼ tsp. baking powder
Pinch of salt

2 eggs
1¼ cups superfine sugar
1 tsp. vanilla extract
4 oz. semisweet chocolate, chopped coarse

Preheat the oven to 350°F (180°C). Line 2 baking sheets with parchment.

Melt the bittersweet chocolate and butter. Allow to cool slightly. Sift the flour, baking powder and salt together. In another bowl, beat the eggs, sugar, and vanilla extract until thick and pale. Stir the melted chocolate into the eggs and sugar, followed by the flour and semisweet chocolate chunks.

Drop tablespoons of mixture onto baking sheets and bake for 8 to 10 minutes. Slide the parchment onto wire racks.

When completely cool, store in an airtight container for 2 to 3 days.

Makes 2 dozen

chocolate whirls

see variations page 158

Pretty little cookies that taste as good as they look.

for the cookies

1 cup (2 sticks) softened sweet butter
½ cup confectioners' sugar
1 oz. bittersweet chocolate, melted
1½ cups all-purpose flour
2 tbsp. Dutch process cocoa powder
3 tbsp. cornstarch

for the filling

4 tbsp. (½ stick) sweet butter
1½ cups confectioners' sugar
1 oz. bittersweet chocolate, melted
2 tbsp. confectioners' sugar

Preheat the oven to 350°F (175°C). Beat the butter and confectioners' sugar together until light and fluffy. Stir in the chocolate. Sift the flour, cocoa powder, and cornstarch and stir into the creamed mixture.

Pipe the mixture using a ¾-in. (1½-cm.) fluted nozzle into 2-in. (5-cm.) rosettes spaced 2 in. (5 cm.) apart on a non-stick baking sheet. Bake for 10 to 12 minutes until golden. Allow to firm up slightly before transferring them to a wire rack to cool. Beat the butter and confectioners' sugar together until light and fluffy and stir in the chocolate. Spread the filling onto the bottom of half the cookies, and then sandwich together with the other halves. Dust with the 2 tablespoons of confectioners' sugar. Store filled cookies in an airtight container for 3 to 4 days and unfilled cookies for 5 to 7 days.

Makes 1½ dozen

triple chocolate cookies

see variations page 159

Rich and full-flavored, these chunky chocolate cookies with dark and white chocolate chips are irresistible.

1 cup all-purpose flour
½ cup unsweetened cocoa powder
½ tsp. baking soda
¼ tsp. baking powder
Pinch of salt
½ cup (1 stick) sweet butter

½ cup granulated sugar
½ cup light brown sugar
1 egg
1 tsp. vanilla extract
½ cup (3 oz.) semisweet chocolate chips
½ cup (3 oz.) white chocolate chips

Preheat the oven to 350°F (160°C). Sift together the flour, cocoa powder, baking soda, baking powder, and salt. Set aside. Beat the butter and sugar until smooth and creamy, and beat in the egg and vanilla extract. Add the flour mixture and mix until almost blended. Add the chocolate chips, and mix.

Scoop the dough onto a baking sheet 2 in. (5 cm.) apart. If preparing dough ahead, roll the dough into a log 1½ in. (4 cm.) thick, wrap in foil, and refrigerate for 2 hours. Before baking, cut the log into ¼-in. (6-mm.) slices and place the slices 1½ in. (4 cm.) apart on a non-stick baking sheet. Bake for 12 to 14 minutes.

Transfer to a wire rack to cool, and store in an airtight container for 5 to 7 days.

Makes 3 dozen

variations

dalmatian bars

see base recipe page 127

cherry dalmatian bars
Prepare the basic cookie dough and substitute ½ cup (3 oz.) whole candied cherries for ½ cup (3 oz.) of the white chocolate chips.

double chocolate dalmatian bars
Prepare the basic cookie dough and substitute (3 oz.) semisweet chocolate for the bittersweet chocolate.

chocolate orange dalmatian bars
Prepare the basic cookie dough and add the grated zest of 1 orange (2 to 3 teaspoons) to the butter and sugar mixture.

variations

cream cheese & chocolate double deckers

see base recipe page 128

cream cheese, walnut, & chocolate double deckers
Prepare the basic cookie dough and add ½ cup (2 oz.) coarsely chopped walnuts to the batter.

cream cheese & white chocolate double deckers
Prepare the basic cookie dough and add ½ cup (3 oz.) white chocolate chips to the batter.

cream cheese, raisin, & chocolate double deckers
Prepare the basic cookie dough and add ½ cup (3 oz.) raisins to the batter.

white chocolate chunk cookies

see base recipe page 131

white chocolate chunk & raisin cookies
Prepare the basic cookie dough and add ½ cup (3 oz.) raisins with the white chocolate chunks.

dark-dipped white chocolate chunk cookies
Prepare the basic cookie dough. When the cookies are baked and cool, dip half of each cookie in melted chocolate and place on parchment until the chocolate is set.

white chocolate chunk & pecan cookies
Prepare the basic cookie dough and add ½ cup (2 oz.) chopped pecans with the white chocolate chunks.

variations

chocolate-drizzled ginger cookies

see base recipe page 132

lemon chocolate-drizzled cookies
Prepare the basic cookie dough, substituting the grated zest of 2 lemons
(4 to 6 teaspoons) for the ground ginger. Add the lemon zest to the egg
and sugar mixture.

cinnamon chocolate-drizzled cookies
Prepare the basic cookie dough, substituting ground cinnamon for the
ground ginger.

vanilla chocolate-drizzled cookies
Prepare the basic cookie dough, substituting 2 teaspoons vanilla extract for
the ground ginger.

marbled chocolate & vanilla cookies

see base recipe page 135

chocolate orange-marbled cookies
Prepare the basic cookie dough, then add grated zest of 1 orange
(2 to 4 teaspoons) and ⅛ teaspoon orange food color to one half of
the dough. Marble the doughs together in the same way.

chocolate mint-marbled cookies
Prepare the basic cookie dough, then add ⅛ teaspoon green food color and
add ¼ teaspoon peppermint extract to one half of the dough. Marble the
doughs together in the same way.

chocolate raspberry-marbled cookies
Prepare the basic cookie dough, then add ⅛ teaspoon red food color and
¼ teaspoon raspberry flavor to one half of the dough. Marble the doughs
together in the same way.

variations

chocolate shortbread

see base recipe page 136

chocolate & orange shortbread
Prepare the basic cookie dough, adding the grated zest of 1 orange
(2 to 3 teaspoons) to the butter and sugar.

chocolate chip shortbread
Prepare the basic cookie dough, adding 1 cup (5 oz.) semisweet chocolate
chips when the dough starts to clump together.

chocolate & ginger shortbread
Prepare the basic cookie dough, adding 3 tablespoons chopped candied
ginger when the dough starts to clump together.

variations

chocolate spice cookies

see base recipe page 137

chocolate pecan spice cookies
Prepare the basic cookie dough and add ½ cup (2 oz.) coarsely
chopped pecans.

chocolate cinnamon maple cookies
Prepare the basic cookie dough and substitute cinnamon for the allspice.

chocolate ginger cookies
Prepare the basic cookie dough and substitute ginger for the allspice,
and molasses for the maple syrup.

variations

chocolate & orange sandwich cookies

see base recipe page 139

chocolate & orange sandwich cookies with vanilla cream filling
Prepare the basic cookie dough and substitute 2 teaspoons vanilla extract for the grated orange zest and juice in the filling.

chocolate & orange sandwich cookies with mocha filling
Prepare the basic cookie dough and substitute 2 teaspoons instant coffee powder for the grated orange zest and juice in the filling. Dissolve the coffee in 1 tablespoon hot water first.

chocolate mint sandwich cookies with chocolate filling
Prepare the basic cookie dough, then substitute ¼ teaspoon peppermint extract for the grated orange zest in the cookies and 1 tablespoon Dutch process cocoa powder dissolved in 1 tablespoon hot water for the grated orange zest and juice in the filling.

variations

chocolate pinwheels

see base recipe page 140

mocha pinwheels
Prepare the basic cookie dough, adding the chocolate to one half of the dough, and 2 teaspoons instant coffee powder dissolved in 1 tablespoon hot water to the other half.

raspberry & lemon pinwheels
Prepare the basic cookie dough, substituting 2 teaspoons raspberry flavor and ½ teaspoon pink food color for the chocolate in one half of the dough. In the other half, add the grated zest of 1 lemon (2 to 3 teaspoons) and ½ teaspoon yellow food color.

chocolate & lemon pinwheels
Prepare the basic cookie dough, adding the chocolate to one half of the dough, and grated zest of 1 lemon (2 to 3 teaspoons) and ½ teaspoon yellow food color to the other half.

variations

chocolate fingers

see base recipe page 141

mega chocolate fingers

Prepare the basic cookie dough, substituting 2 tablespoons cocoa powder for an equal amount of the flour. Add ½ cup (3 oz.) semisweet chocolate chips into the mixture before spreading it into the pan.

peanut chocolate fingers

Prepare the basic cookie dough, substituting 2 tablespoons cocoa powder for an equal amount of the flour, and stir in all the melted chocolate. When baked, spread with 1 cup (8 oz.) smooth peanut butter and top with the pecans and ½ cup (3 oz.) butterscotch chips.

chocolate banana fingers

Prepare the basic cookie dough and add 1 mashed banana to the mixture. Bake and top with the pecans and ½ cup (2 oz.) banana chips.

variations

chewy chocolate cookies

see base recipe page 142

chewy chocolate walnut cookies
Prepare the basic cookie dough and add ½ cup (2 oz.) coarsely chopped walnuts.

chewy chocolate cherry cookies
Prepare the basic cookie dough and add ½ cup (3 oz.) chopped natural candied cherries.

chewy chocolate and raisin cookies
Prepare the basic cookie dough and add ½ cup (3 oz.) raisins.

variations

chocolate whirls

see base recipe page 145

dipped chocolate whirls
Prepare the basic cookie dough and then half-dip the filled cookies in tempered bittersweet chocolate.

chocolate & ginger whirls
Prepare the basic cookie dough, adding 1 teaspoon ground ginger to the flour and 2 tablespoons chopped candied ginger to the filling.

chocolate cinnamon & raisin whirls
Prepare the basic cookie dough, adding 1 teaspoon ground cinnamon to the flour and 2 tablespoons raisins to the filling.

variations

triple chocolate cookies

see base recipe page 146

peppermint chocolate chip cookies
Prepare the basic dark cookie dough using half the quantity of cocoa powder. Add ¼ teaspoon peppermint extract and 1 cup (5 oz.) semisweet chocolate chips.

walnut chip cookies
Prepare the basic dark cookie dough using half the quantity of cocoa powder; then add ½ cup (3½ oz.) chopped walnuts and ½ cup (3 oz.) semisweet chocolate chips.

dark chocolate cherry cookies
Prepare the basic dark cookie dough. Add ½ cup (3 oz.) chopped candied cherries and ½ cup (3 oz.) bittersweet chocolate chips.

celebration cookies

Cookies are an ideal way to mark a special occasion — use these recipes to concoct heart-shaped cookies for Valentine's Day or fortune cookies to usher in the Chinese New Year, or bake traditional Rugelach and Christmas shortbread.

christmas tree cookies

see variations page 182

These cookies are a great — and inexpensive — holiday gift idea.

1 ¼ cups all-purpose flour
½ tsp. baking powder
Pinch of salt
½ cup (1 stick) sweet butter
½ cup superfine sugar

1 egg
1 tsp. vanilla extract
1 egg white
3 tbsp. green sugar crystals

Preheat the oven to 350°F (175°C). Sift the flour, baking powder, and salt together. Beat the butter and sugar until smooth, add the egg and vanilla, and stir in the dry ingredients. Mix the dough with your hands.

Put ½ cup of dough to one side and divide the remainder in half. Roll into 2 logs about 2 in. (5 cm.) thick. Gently press each log into a triangular shape. Wrap and refrigerate the logs and the extra dough until firm. Cut the triangular logs into ¼-in.- (6-mm.-) thick slices and lay them 2 in. (5 cm.) apart on baking sheets. Mold the excess dough into tree-trunk shapes and attach to achieve a Christmas tree shape. Alternately, use a tree-shaped cookie cutter.

Brush each Christmas tree cookie with egg white and sprinkle with the sugar crystals. Bake for 8 to 10 minutes until golden. Remove onto wire racks and allow to cool. Decorate with royal icing and candies. Store in an airtight container for 4 to 5 days.

Makes 1 dozen

cinnamon stars

see variations page 183

These cookies can be made to accompany almost any celebration — just change the decoration according to the occasion.

2 scant cups ground almonds
1 tsp. ground cinnamon
1 cup superfine sugar
½ egg white

2 tbsp. confectioners' sugar, to dust
    work surface
Royal icing, candies, and colored sugar crystals,
    to decorate

Preheat the oven to 300°F (150°C). Line 2 baking sheets with parchment. Mix together the ground almonds, cinnamon, and sugar. Add the egg white and water and work to a smooth dough with your hands.

Roll out the dough on a surface dusted with confectioners' sugar to ¼ in. (6 mm.) thick. Cut out stars using a star-shaped cookie cutter. Place the cookies on the baking sheets and bake for 30 to 35 minutes.

Transfer to wire racks and allow to cool. Pipe or spread with royal icing and decorate with candies and colored sugar crystals.

Makes 1½ dozen

easter chocolate nest cookies

see variations page 184

Kids will love these, and they taste as good as they look!

½ cup (1 stick) sweet butter
½ cup superfine sugar
½ cup unrefined light brown sugar
2 eggs
1 tsp. vanilla extract
2 tbsp. (1 oz.) bittersweet chocolate, melted
1⅓ cups all-purpose flour

2 tbsp. Dutch process cocoa powder
¼ tsp. baking soda
Pinch of salt
1 cup flaked coconut
¾ cup rolled oats
2 cups (7 oz.) candy coated eggs

Preheat the oven to 350°F (175°C). Grease 2 baking sheets. Beat the butter and sugars. Add the eggs, vanilla extract, and melted chocolate, and beat until smooth.

Sift the flour, Dutch process cocoa powder, baking soda, and salt together and stir into the butter mixture. Stir the coconut and oats into the batter and mix to combine. Drop spoonfuls onto baking sheets and shape into small rounds about 2 in. (5 cm.) in diameter. Using a floured thumb, make a 1 in. (2 cm.) impression in each cookie. Bake for 10 to 12 minutes.

Transfer to wire racks to cool. When completely cool, fill with the candy-coated eggs.

Store in an airtight container for 4 to 5 days.

Makes 2 dozen

valentine heart cookies

see variations page 185

For a sweeter valentine gift, make personalized valentine cookies instead of cards.

¾ cup (1½ sticks) sweet butter
1 cup confectioners' sugar
1½ tsp. vanilla extract
2½ cups all-purpose flour, sifted

1 egg
1 egg yolk
Royal icing, red and pink food-color, to decorate

Line 2 baking sheets with parchment. Combine the butter, sugar, and vanilla extract in a food processor until smooth.

Add the flour, egg, and egg yolk and process to a smooth dough. Wrap in parchment and refrigerate until firm.

Preheat the oven to 350°F (175°C). Roll out the dough either on a lightly floured work surface or between 2 sheets of parchment to ¼ in. (6 mm.) thick.

Cut out cookies using heart-shaped cutters. Place the cookies on the sheets and bake for 10 to 12 minutes. Cool on wire racks. Decorate with the royal icing. Store in an airtight container for 5 to 7 days.

Makes 2 dozen

lovers' knots

see variations page 186

Not just for lovers! Make these for friends and family — they're sure to be appreciated.

1 cup all-purpose flour
½ tsp. baking powder
Pinch of salt
1 tbsp. (⅛ stick) sweet butter
2 tbsp. superfine sugar

Grated zest of 1 lemon
1 egg
1½ tbsp. rum
2 tbsp. confectioners' sugar

Sift the flour, baking powder, and salt into a bowl. Cut in the butter and then add the sugar and lemon zest. Stir in the egg and rum and work the mixture until it forms a smooth dough. Turn onto a floured surface and knead the dough. Cover and let stand for 30 minutes.

Divide the dough in half, cover one half in parchment, and roll out the other half to 12 x 3 in. (31 x 8 cm.). Cut the rectangle into ½-in. (1-cm.) strips and tie each strip loosely into a knot. Put to one side and repeat using the remaining dough.

Heat a deep fat fryer to 375°F (190°C) and deep-fry the dough in small batches until golden. Remove with a slotted spoon, drain on kitchen towels, and dust with confectioners' sugar. Serve while still warm.

Makes 2 dozen

lebkuchen

see variations page 187

Classic German spiced honey biscuits are very popular, especially at Christmas time.

for the cookies

1 egg
¾ cup light brown sugar
½ cup honey
½ cup molasses
3 cups all-purpose flour
1¼ tsp. ground nutmeg
1¼ tsp. ground cinnamon
½ tsp. ground cloves
½ tsp. ground allspice

for the glaze

1½ cups confectioners' sugar
1 tbsp. egg white
1 tbsp. lemon juice
Grated zest 1 lemon

Grease 3 baking sheets. Beat the egg and sugar together until light and fluffy. Stir in the honey and molasses. Sift the flour and spices and stir into the egg mixture. Chill until firm, for about 2 hours or overnight. Preheat the oven to 350°F (175°C). Roll out to ¼ in. (6 mm.) thick and cut into 3 x 2 in. (8 x 5 cm.) rectangles. Bake for 10 to 12 minutes.

Transfer to a wire rack. Mix the confectioners' sugar, egg white, lemon juice, and lemon zest together and brush this glaze over the cookies.

Allow the glaze to firm, then store the cookies in an airtight container for 4 to 5 days.

Makes 1½ dozen

rugelach

see variations page 188

These Jewish pastries are classic cookies for the festival of Channukah. Make sure the kitchen isn't too warm when you're making the dough, or it may prove troublesome.

for the cookies

1 cup (2 sticks) sweet butter
1 cup (9 oz.) cream cheese
2½ cups all-purpose flour

for the filling

¾ cup superfine sugar
½ cup (3 oz.) raisins
1 tsp. ground cinnamon
1 scant cup (3½ oz.) ground almonds

Beat the butter and cream cheese together until smooth. Beat in the flour a little at a time. Knead the dough lightly until the flour is incorporated. Refrigerate until the dough is firm. While the dough is chilling, make the filling. Mix together ½ cup of the sugar, the raisins, cinnamon, and almonds. Roll out half the dough between 2 pieces of lightly-floured plastic. Work quickly, as the dough becomes hard to manage as it warms up. Roll to a rectangle and cut triangles the size of pie wedges from the dough, with sides slightly longer than the base. Repeat with the remaining half of the dough.

Preheat the oven to 350°F (175°C). Spread a little of the filling on top of the dough wedges and roll up toward the point. Place on baking sheets with the point tucked under the roll. Sprinkle with sugar and bake for 15 to 18 minutes until golden. Serve hot or cold. Store in an airtight container for 3 to 5 days.

Makes 3 dozen

giant pumpkin cookies

see variations page 189

Ghosts, witches, and cats are all part of Halloween — and now so are pumpkin cookies.

for the cookies

1¾ cups all-purpose flour
1 tsp. baking powder
½ tsp. salt
½ cup (1 stick) sweet butter
½ cup superfine sugar
2 eggs
1 tsp. vanilla extract

for the icing

2 cups confectioners' sugar
¼ cup milk
Orange and black food color
Royal icing, to decorate
Orange and green sugar crystals

Preheat the oven to 350°F (175°C). Sift the flour, baking powder, and salt together in a bowl. In a separate bowl, beat the butter and sugar and add the eggs and vanilla. Stir the dry ingredients to form a smooth dough. Wrap the dough in parchment and refrigerate until firm.

Cut the dough in half and roll out each piece on a lightly floured sheet of parchment to ¼ in. (6 mm.) thick. Cut out a large pumpkin shape either freehand, or use a stencil cut from thickened card or plastic. Lift onto a baking sheet. Bake for 12 to 15 minutes until golden. Cool on a baking sheet and transfer to a wire rack. When completely cool, combine the icing ingredients, and decorate. Store in an airtight container for 5 to 7 days.

Makes 2 to 4

layered birthday cookie

see variations page 190

Create your own extravagant birthday alternative for a cookie lover.

for the cookie

1 cup (2 sticks) sweet butter
2 cups light brown sugar
2 eggs
2 tsp. vanilla extract
3 cups all-purpose flour
6 tbsp. Dutch process cocoa powder
1 tsp. baking soda

for the topping

½ cup (1 stick) sweet butter
2 cups confectioners' sugar
1 cup (9 oz.) cream cheese
1 cup (8 oz.) melted bittersweet chocolate
½ cup (3 oz.) candies
½ cup (3 oz.) semisweet
    chocolate chips

Preheat the oven to 350°F (175°C). Line two 11-in. (28-cm.) springform pans with parchment.

Beat the butter and sugar together. Add the eggs and vanilla extract. Sift the flour, Dutch process cocoa powder and baking soda and stir into the batter. Divide the dough in two, and press into the prepared pans. Bake for 20 minutes until golden. Remove from the oven and allow to cool, then transfer to a wire rack.

To prepare the topping, beat the butter and confectioners' sugar together, then beat in the cream cheese and melted chocolate. Spread the topping over the cooled cookies, place one on top of the other, decorate, and top with chocolate chips and candies.

Makes 1 large cookie

witches' hats

see variations page 191

For visiting ghosts and ghouls on All Hallows' Eve.

2 cups all-purpose flour
½ tsp. baking powder
Pinch of salt
½ cup (1 stick) sweet butter

1 cup superfine sugar
1 egg
2 tsp. vanilla extract
Royal icing and food colors, to decorate.

Line 2 baking sheets with parchment. Sift the flour, baking powder, and salt into a bowl. In a separate bowl, beat the butter and sugar until light and fluffy. Add the egg and vanilla. Stir in the flour mixture until incorporated, and knead lightly until combined. Divide the dough in half, flatten each half into a patty, wrap in parchment, and refrigerate until firm.

Preheat the oven to 350°F (175°C). Roll out the dough between two lightly floured plastic sheets or parchment to ⅛ in. (3 mm.) thick. Using a floured witch's hat cutter or a plastic stencil, cut out cookies and put onto the baking sheets 1½ in. (4 cm.) apart. Bake for 8 to 10 minutes.

Slide the parchment onto wire racks and allow the cookies to cool. Decorate with royal icing.

Store in an airtight container for 5 to 7 days.

Makes 2 dozen

fortune cookies

see variations page 192

Write your own fortunes and enclose them in the fold of these crunchy Chinese cookies.

2 to 3 egg whites
½ cup superfine sugar
Pinch of salt
¼ tsp. vanilla extract

1 cup all-purpose flour
Pinch of ground star anise
½ cup melted sweet butter
2 tbsp. water

Line 2 baking sheets with parchment. Beat together the egg whites, sugar, and salt. Stir in the vanilla, flour, and star anise. Add the butter and water and mix to a smooth paste.

Refrigerate for approximately 30 minutes, until the mixture is set. Preheat the oven to 350°F (175°C). Spread small amounts of the mixture onto the parchment to form 3-in. (8-cm.) circles, 1½ in. (4 cm.) apart. Bake for 3 to 4 minutes, until the edges start to brown.

Carefully remove one cookie at a time with a palette knife. Turn upside down, place the fortune paper inside, and fold in half. Pinch in the middle and fold again to give a fortune cookie shape. Put to one side to cool and harden. If they become too hard, return the cookies to the oven for a few seconds.

Store in an airtight container for 5 to 7 days.

Makes 2 dozen

gumdrop party cookies

see variations page 193

These are the Martini of the cookie world — any time, any place, anywhere — just decorate with different colored gumdrops. For Christmas, use red and green and for Halloween, orange and black.

2⅓ cups all-purpose flour
1 tsp. baking soda
Pinch of salt
1 cup (2 sticks) unsalted butter
1 cup superfine sugar

½ cup light brown sugar
2 eggs
1 tsp. vanilla
1 cup gumdrops, snipped with floured scissors

Preheat the oven to 350°F (175°C). Sift the flour, baking soda, and salt together in a bowl.

Beat the butter and sugars until light and fluffy, then add the eggs and vanilla. Stir in the dry ingredients and gumdrops.

Drop spoonfuls onto baking sheets and bake for 12 to 15 minutes.

Transfer to wire racks to cool. When completely cool, store in an airtight container for 3 to 4 days.

Makes 2 dozen

variations

christmas tree cookies

see base recipe page 161

christmas stars
Prepare the basic cookie dough and refrigerate until firm. Roll out the dough to ¼ in. (6 mm.) thick and cut out star shapes using a large star-shaped cutter. Brush with egg white and sprinkle with different colored sugar crystals. Bake, cool, and decorate with candies.

christmas angels
Prepare the basic cookie dough and refrigerate until firm. Roll out the dough to ¼ in. (6 mm.) thick and cut out angel shapes using a large angel-shaped cutter. Brush with egg white and sprinkle with different colored sugar crystals. Bake, cool, and decorate with candies.

variations

cinnamon stars

see base recipe page 162

sandwich stars
Prepare the basic cookie dough. Roll the dough out to ⅛ in. (3 mm.) thick and cut out the stars. Bake, cool, fill with your favorite icing, and sandwich together.

cherry stars
Prepare the basic cookie dough and add ¼ cup (2 oz.) dried cherries to the mix once it has formed a smooth dough.

chocolate chip cinnamon stars
Prepare the basic cookie dough and add ¼ cup (2 oz.) semisweet chocolate chips to the mix once it has formed a smooth dough.

variations

easter chocolate nest cookies

see base recipe page 165

chocolate & cherry easter nest cookies
Prepare the basic cookie dough and add ½ cup (3 oz.) chopped red candied cherries to the mixture with the coconut and oats.

chocolate & raisin easter nest cookies
Prepare the basic cookie dough and add ½ cup (3 oz.) raisins to the mixture with coconut and oats.

double chocolate easter nest cookies
Prepare the basic cookie dough and add ½ cup (3 oz.) white chocolate chips to the mixture with the coconut and oats.

variations

valentine heart cookies

see base recipe page 166

lemon valentine cookies
Prepare the basic cookie dough and add the grated zest of 1 lemon
(2 to 3 teaspoons) to the mixture.

chocolate valentine cookies
Prepare the basic cookie dough, substituting 2 tablespoons Dutch process
cocoa powder for 2 tablespoons of the all-purpose flour.

hazelnut valentine cookies
Prepare the basic cookie dough, substituting ½ cup (2½ oz.) toasted ground
hazelnuts for the same amount of flour.

variations

lovers' knots

see base recipe page 169

orange lovers' knots
Prepare the basic cookie dough but substitute dry white wine for the rum, and orange zest for the lemon zest.

chocolate & cinnamon lovers' knots
Prepare the basic cookie dough but substitute 2 tablespoons cocoa powder for 2 tablespoons flour and 2 tablespoons superfine sugar. Add 1 teaspoon ground cinnamon to the confectioners' sugar. Toss the fried cookies in the cinnamon sugar. Serve immediately.

variations

lebkuchen

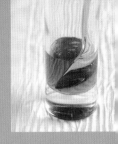

see base recipe page 170

candied lemon lebkuchen
Prepare the basic cookie dough and add ½ cup (3 oz.) finely chopped candied
lemon peel.

nutty lebkuchen
Prepare the basic cookie dough and add ½ cup (2 oz.) coarsely chopped
pecan nuts.

golden lebkuchen
Prepare the basic cookie dough, but substitute maple syrup for the molasses.

variations

rugelach

see base recipe page 171

lemon rugelach
Prepare the basic cookie dough and fill with a mixture of ½ cup lemon curd and ½ cup (2 oz.) ground almonds.

strawberry rugelach
Prepare the basic cookie dough and fill with a mixture of ½ cup strawberry jam and ½ cup (2 oz.) ground almonds.

pecan rugelach
Prepare the basic cookie dough and substitute coarsely chopped pecans for the ground almonds.

giant pumpkin cookies

see base recipe page 173

spiced pumpkin cookies
Prepare the basic cookie dough and add ½ teaspoon ground cinnamon and
¼ teaspoon ground allspice to the dough. Cut out smaller cookies, and bake
for 8 to 10 minutes. Decorate as for main recipe.

raisin pumpkin cookies
Prepare the basic cookie dough and add ½ cup (3 oz.) raisins to the dough.

cream cheese-topped pumpkin cookies
Beat ½ cup (4½ oz.) cream cheese with 1 cup confectioners' sugar and the
grated zest of 1 lemon (2 to 3 teaspoons). Prepare the basic cookie dough
and spread the cooled cookies with the cream cheese icing and colored
sugar crystals.

variations

layered birthday cookie

see base recipe page 174

marshmallow layered cookie
Prepare the basic cookie dough and substitute 1 cup pink marshmallow icing for the cream cheese and bittersweet chocolate and miniature marshmallows for the candies and chocolate chips.

fresh & fruity cookie cake
Prepare the basic cookie dough, omitting the cocoa powder. Substitute 2 cups heavy cream for all of the filling ingredients. Whip and sweeten the heavy cream with 2 teaspoons vanilla extract and 2 tablespoons confectioners' sugar. Spread the cream on top of the cookies and top both with fresh halved strawberries, raspberries, and blueberries.

variations

witches' hats

see base recipe page 177

black cats
Prepare the basic recipe and cut out cookies using a Halloween cat-shaped cutter. Decorate the cookies with black, white, and silver decorations.

ghosts
Prepare the basic recipe and cut out cookies using a Halloween ghost-shaped cutter. Decorate the cookies with white, silver, and red decorations.

cobwebs
Prepare the basic recipe and cut out cookies using a Halloween cobweb or round cutter. Decorate the cookies with white icing, pipe circles of a darker color, and drag the icing to create a cobweb effect.

variations

fortune cookies

see base recipe page 178

chocolate fortune cookies
Prepare the basic cookie dough and substitute 1 tablespoon Dutch process cocoa powder for the same amount of flour.

almond fortune cookies
Prepare the basic cookie dough and substitute almond extract for the vanilla extract.

ginger fortune cookies
Prepare the basic cookie dough and add ½ teaspoon ground ginger to the flour.

variations

gumdrop party cookies

see base recipe page 181

chocolate gumdrop cookies
Prepare the basic cookie dough and substitute 2 tablespoons Dutch process cocoa powder for the same amount of flour.

spicy gumdrop cookies
Prepare the basic cookie dough and add 1½ teaspoons ground ginger and ½ teaspoon ground nutmeg to the dough.

lemon gumdrop cookies
Prepare the basic cookie dough and add the grated zest of 2 lemons (4 to 6 teaspoons).

wholesome healthy cookies

Not all cookies and bars need to be bad for you —
they can be low in fat, or packed with wholesome
dried fruit and healthy oats. Date bars are moist with
the goodness of natural sugar, and fig and walnut
bites contain natural fats that are kind to the body.

granola seed & nut bar

see variations page 215

Great for breakfast on the run, or as an energy snack at any time of day, these nutty bars are packed full of flavor.

½ cup (1 stick) sweet butter
½ cup unrefined light brown sugar
¼ cup corn syrup
1 heaped cup rolled oats

½ cup granola
2 tbsp. (1 oz.) sesame seeds
2 tbsp. (1 oz.) sunflower seeds
¼ cup (1¼ oz.) chopped almonds

Preheat the oven to 375°F (190°C). Line a 7-in.- (18-cm.-) square baking tray with parchment. Melt the butter, sugar, and syrup in a pan over low heat.

Pulse the rolled oats in a food processor for 30 seconds. Stir the oats, seeds, and almonds into the melted butter, syrup, and sugar. Spread the mixture into the lined tray and level the surface with a palette knife.

Bake for 10 to 12 minutes until golden. Remove from the oven and cool in the pan for at least 1 hour. Remove from pan and slice into bars.

Store in an airtight container for 5 to 7 days.

Makes 1 dozen

sticky date bars

see variations page 216

Dates provide a quick sugar boost, so these bars are an immediate energy source.

1½ cups (9 oz.) pitted and chopped dried dates
Grated zest (2 to 3 tsp.) and juice (3 tbsp.) of
    1 orange
¾ cup (1½ sticks) sweet butter

1½ cups all-purpose flour
2 tbsp. cornstarch
½ tsp. baking powder
¼ cup unrefined light brown sugar

Preheat the oven to 375°F (190°C). Grease and line an 8 x 9-in. (20 x 23-cm.) pan. Put the dates, orange zest, and juice in a pan, and add ½ cup boiling water. Cook the dates for 3 to 4 minutes until soft, stirring all the time to make sure they don't stick. Remove from the heat. Spoon onto a plate and allow to cool.

Cut the butter into the sifted flour, cornstarch, and baking powder, along with the sugar. Press two-thirds of the mixture into the base of the greased and lined pan.

Process the dates in a blender for 30 seconds until smooth, and spread over the base in the pan. Sprinkle the remaining one-third of the mixture over the pan, pressing down lightly to give a crumbled effect. Bake for 30 to 35 minutes. Slice into bars and remove from the pan when cool.

Store in an airtight container for 4 to 5 days.

Makes 2 dozen

pumpkin cookies

see variations page 217

These moist spicy cookies are low in fat and very simple to make.

¾ cup pumpkin puree
½ cup fat-free plain yogurt
1 tsp. vanilla extract
2 cups all-purpose flour
1 tsp. ground cinnamon
½ tsp. ground ginger

½ tsp. ground allspice
½ tsp. ground nutmeg
½ tsp. baking soda
1 cup (5 oz.) raisins
¾ cup unrefined light brown sugar

Preheat the oven to 350°F (175°C). Grease 2 baking sheets. Mix together pumpkin puree, yogurt, and vanilla.

In a separate bowl sift the flour, spices, and baking soda. Add the raisins and sugar. Stir the dry ingredients into the pumpkin mixture, and blend until smooth.

Drop spoonfuls onto baking sheets 2 in. (5 cm.) apart. Bake for 12 to 15 minutes until firm. Cool on wire racks.

When completely cool, store in an airtight container for 4 to 5 days.

Makes 3½ dozen

apricot flapjack

see variations page 218

These flapjacks aren't just a tasty treat — apricots and oats are both slow-release carbohydrates, meaning this bar will keep your hunger at bay.

1½ cups (3 sticks) sweet butter
5 tbsp. maple syrup
1½ cups unrefined light brown sugar
4½ cups rolled oats
1 cup (7oz.) chopped dried apricots

Preheat the oven to 375°F (190°C). Grease and line an 8 x 12-in. (20 x 30-cm.) pan. Melt the butter, maple syrup, and sugar in a pan.

Stir in the oats and chopped apricots. Spoon the mixture into the pan, and bake for 15 to 20 minutes.

Remove from the oven, and allow to cool completely before cutting into squares.

Store in an airtight container for 5 to 7 days.

Makes 1½ dozen

cherry & oatmeal cookies

see variations page 219

Chewy cherries give this cookie a superb texture. The unrefined light brown sugar and cinnamon give it a sweet and slightly spicy flavor.

¼ cup (½ stick) sweet butter
½ cup unrefined light brown sugar
1 egg
¼ cup sour cream
1 tsp. vanilla extract
¾ cup all-purpose flour

¼ tsp. baking soda
Pinch of salt
¼ tsp. ground cinnamon
½ cup oatmeal
1 cup (5 oz.) dried cherries

Preheat the oven to 350°F (175°C). In a large bowl, beat the butter and sugar together. Add the egg.

Beat in the sour cream and vanilla extract, and stir in the dry ingredients and cherries.

Drop spoonfuls of the mixture onto non-stick baking sheets. Bake for 12 to 15 minutes. Cool for 5 minutes before removing from the sheets.

Store in an airtight container for 5 to 7 days.

Makes 2 dozen

macadamia nut cookies

see variations page 220

Bite-sized, crisp, and nutty — these cookies will disappear quicker than you think.

1 cup (5 oz.) macadamia nuts
2 to 3 tbsp. milk
¾ cup unrefined light brown sugar
1 egg
1 tsp. vanilla extract

1 cup all-purpose flour
¼ tsp. baking soda
¼ tsp. ground nutmeg
Pinch of salt
½ cup granulated sugar

Preheat the oven to 350°F (175°C). Put the macadamia nuts and milk into a food processor and blend for about 2 minutes, or until smooth. Spoon the mixture into a large bowl and add the sugar, egg, and vanilla. Beat well.

Sift the flour, baking soda, nutmeg, and salt and stir into the nut mixture to form a smooth paste.

Roll the mixture into balls and dip them into the granulated sugar. Put onto baking sheets and flatten slightly with a fork to give a criss-cross effect. Bake for 8 to 10 minutes until golden. Transfer to wire racks to cool.

When completely cool, store in an airtight container 5 to 7 days.

Makes 1½ dozen

granola cookies

see variations page 221

Packed full of fruits and nuts, these cookies make a great morning snack to tide you over until lunch.

1 cup (2 sticks) sweet butter
1½ cups unrefined light brown sugar
2 eggs
1 cup malted milk powder
2 cups all-purpose flour

½ tsp. baking soda
¾ cup granola
½ cup (2 oz.) chopped walnuts
½ cup (3 oz.) raisins

Preheat the oven to 350ºF (175ºC).

Beat the butter and sugar in a bowl until fluffy. Add the eggs.

Add the dry ingredients, then stir in the dried fruit. Mix until combined.

Roll the dough into walnut-sized balls, place them on a non-stick baking sheet, and press with a fork to flatten them. Bake for 15 to 18 minutes, or until golden.

Store in an airtight container for 5 to 7 days.

Makes 3 dozen

fig & walnut bites

see variations page 222

Sweetened with unrefined maple syrup and fruit, these cookies are a wholesome antidote to a wicked sugar craving.

3 cups (15 oz.) walnuts
1½ cups (3 sticks) sweet butter
¾ cup maple syrup
1 egg

1 tsp. vanilla extract
1½ cups all-purpose flour
1 cup (5 oz.) finely chopped figs

Preheat the oven to 350°F (175°C). Put the walnuts on a tray and toast in the oven for 4 to 5 minutes. Allow to cool. Beat the butter and maple syrup until light and fluffy. Add the egg and vanilla. Stir in the flour.

Put the walnuts in a food processor and blend until finely ground. Add the walnuts and figs to the dough, and stir to incorporate.

Roll the dough into balls. Place 1½ in. (4 cm.) apart on 2 baking sheets and flatten slightly with a fork. Bake for 12 to 15 minutes until golden. Cool on baking sheets before transferring to wire racks.

When completely cool, store in an airtight container for 4 to 5 days.

Makes 3 dozen

apple & prune bars

see variations page 223

Full-flavored and fruity, these bars make ideal low-fat lunch treats.

1 egg
2 egg whites
1 cup unrefined light brown sugar
3 tbsp. safflower oil
1 tsp. vanilla extract
1½ cups all-purpose flour

1 tsp. ground cinnamon
1 tsp. baking soda
Pinch of salt
1½ cups rolled oats
1 cup (5 oz.) chopped pitted prunes
½ cup (2 oz.) chopped dried apple

Preheat the oven to 375°F (190°C). Line a 9 x 13-in. (23 x 33-cm.) pan with parchment. Put the egg, egg whites, and sugar in a food processor, and blend until smooth. Add the oil and vanilla, and process for 20 seconds to incorporate.

Add the flour, cinnamon, baking soda, and salt and process until blended. Add the oats and process for 10 seconds. Remove the mixture to a bowl, and mix in the prunes and apple with a fork.

Spread the dough into the pan and level the surface. Bake for 20 to 25 minutes until a toothpick inserted in the center comes out clean. Cool in the pan.

Slice into bars and store in an airtight container for 4 to 5 days.

Makes 2 dozen

sesame seed cookies

see variations page 224

Toasted sesame seeds give these cookies their wholesome touch, as well as their crunch.

½ cup (5 oz.) sesame seeds
⅓ cup (¾ stick) sweet butter
¾ cup unrefined light brown sugar
1 egg

1 tsp. vanilla extract
½ cup all-purpose flour
Pinch of baking powder
Pinch of salt

Preheat the oven to 375°F (190°C). Grease several baking sheets. Put the sesame seeds on a baking sheet and toast in the oven for 4 to 5 minutes, or until golden.

Beat the butter and sugar until light and fluffy. Add the egg and vanilla.

Sift the flour, baking powder, and salt and stir into the butter mixture. Stir in the sesame seeds. Drop small spoonfuls 1½ in. (4 cm.) apart onto baking sheets and bake for 4 to 6 minutes until golden. Cool for a few minutes on the sheets before transferring to wire racks.

Store in an airtight container 5 to 7 days.

Makes 3 dozen

applesauce cookies

see variations page 225

This reduced-sugar cookie relies on the natural sweetness of apples to save adding extra sugar. The applesauce also helps to make them moist.

½ cup (1 stick) sweet butter
¼ cup unrefined light brown sugar
1 egg
2 cups all-purpose flour, sifted
1 tsp. baking powder, sifted

½ tsp. ground cinnamon, sifted
½ tsp. baking soda, sifted
Pinch of salt
1 cup unsweetened applesauce
2 tbsp. water

Preheat the oven to 350°F (175°C). Beat the butter and sugar in a bowl until light and fluffy. Add the egg.

Stir in the dry ingredients, applesauce, and water one at a time.

Drop teaspoonfuls onto a non-stick baking sheet and bake for 12 to 15 minutes.

Store in an airtight container for 2 to 3 days.

Makes 2½ dozen

berry oat bars

see variations page 226

Use fresh berries for an extra gooey boost; if not, frozen berries will do the trick.

½ cup (1 stick) sweet butter, melted
1⅓ cups unrefined light brown sugar
1⅓ cups all-purpose flour
½ cup rolled oats
2 eggs

½ tsp. baking powder
1 cup (3½ oz.) coconut
½ cup (3 oz.) dried cherries
½ cup (3 oz.) dried blueberries
½ cup (3 oz.) dried strawberries

Preheat the oven to 375°F (190°C). Grease and line an 8 x 12-in. (20 x 30-cm.) pan. Mix butter, ⅓ cup sugar, 1 cup flour, and oats together. Press into the base of the pan.

In another bowl, beat the eggs and remaining sugar until light and fluffy.

Fold the remaining flour, baking powder, coconut, and berries into the egg mixture, and spread over the base. Bake for 20 to 25 minutes until golden.

Store in an airtight container for 2 to 3 days.

Makes 2 dozen

popcorn puffs

see variations page 227

Crunchy and light, these popcorn puffs are quick, simple, and fun to make.

2 cups popcorn
3 egg whites
¼ tsp. cream of tartar

½ cup superfine sugar
½ tsp. baking powder
Pinch of salt

Preheat the oven to 350°F (175°C). Line 2 baking sheets with parchment. Put the popcorn in a food processor and blend for 30 seconds. Put to one side.

Whisk the egg whites and cream of tartar. When soft peaks form, add one-third of the sugar. Whisk for 1 minute, then add another one-third of the sugar. Whisk for a further minute and add the rest of the sugar. Fold the popcorn, baking powder, and salt into the mixture.

Drop spoonfuls onto a baking sheet and bake for 12 to 15 minutes. Transfer the parchment sheets to wire racks. Remove the popcorn puffs when cool.

Store in an airtight container 4 to 5 days.

Makes 1½ dozen

variations

granola seed & nut bar

see base recipe page 195

apricot seed bars
Prepare the basic cookie dough and substitute 4 tablespoons (2 oz.) chopped dried apricots for the chopped almonds.

honey nut bar
Prepare the basic cookie dough and substitute honey for the corn syrup and ½ cup (2 oz.) chopped pecans for the sunflower and sesame seeds.

cranberry & orange breakfast bar
Prepare the basic cookie dough and substitute cranberries for the almonds. Add the grated zest of 1 orange (2 to 3 teaspoons).

variations

sticky date bars

see base recipe page 196

apricot bars
Prepare the basic cookie dough, substituting dried apricots for the dates.

fig & cardamom bars
Prepare the basic cookie dough, adding 2 teaspoons ground cardamom seeds to the flour, and substituting figs for the dates.

blueberry & cherry bars
Prepare the basic cookie dough, substituting dried blueberries and cherries for the dates.

variations

pumpkin cookies

see base recipe page 199

pumpkin cranberry cookies
Prepare the basic cookie dough and substitute ½ cup (3 oz.) dried cranberries
for half of the raisins.

pumpkin apple cookies
Prepare the basic cookie dough and substitute ½ cup (2 oz.) chopped dried
apple for half of the raisins.

pumpkin pecan cookies
Prepare the basic cookie dough and substitute ½ cup (2 oz.) coarsely
chopped pecans for half of the raisins.

variations

apricot flapjack

see base recipe page 200

apricot & chocolate flapjack
Prepare the basic cookie dough and add 6 tablespoons Dutch process cocoa powder to the mixture when adding the oats.

peanut butter flapjack
Prepare the basic cookie dough and add ¼ cup (2 oz.) crunchy peanut butter to the mixture when adding the oats.

ginger flapjack
Prepare the basic cookie dough and add 4 tablespoons (2 oz.) chopped candied ginger to the mixture when adding the oats.

variations

cherry & oatmeal cookies

see base recipe page 201

cherry & walnut oatmeal cookies
Prepare the basic cookie dough and add ½ cup (2 oz.) chopped walnuts.
Decrease the cherries by half.

spiced oatmeal & raisin cookies
Prepare the basic cookie dough and substitute raisins for the cherries. Add
½ teaspoon ground ginger and ¼ teaspoon of allspice.

blueberry & lemon oatmeal cookies
Prepare the basic cookie dough and substitute blueberries for the cherries.
Add the grated zest of 1 lemon (2 to 3 teaspoons).

variations

macadamia nut cookies

see base recipe page 203

macadamia & cranberry cookies
Prepare the basic cookie dough and add ½ cup (3 oz.) dried cranberries after adding the dried ingredients.

macadamia & blueberry cookies
Prepare the basic cookie dough and add ½ cup (3 oz.) dried blueberries after adding the dried ingredients.

pecan & raisin cookies
Prepare the basic cookie dough and substitute pecans for the macadamia nuts. Add ½ cup (3 oz.) raisins after adding the dried ingredients.

variations

granola cookies

see base recipe page 204

granola cookies with apricot & coconut
Prepare the basic cookie dough, substituting chopped dried apricots for
the raisins and ½ cup flaked coconut for the walnuts.

spiced apple granola cookies
Prepare the basic cookie dough, substituting 1 cup flaked coconut
for the raisins, and adding ¼ cup (1 oz.) chopped dried apple
and 1 teaspoon ground cinnamon.

pecan & peach granola cookies
Prepare the basic cookie dough, substituting chopped dried peaches for
the raisins, and pecans for the walnuts.

variations

fig & walnut bites

see base recipe page 207

almond bites
Prepare the basic cookie dough and substitute almonds for the walnuts and omit the figs.

pecan & raisin bites
Prepare the basic cookie dough and substitute pecans for the walnuts and raisins for the figs.

hazelnut & cherry bites
Prepare the basic cookie dough and substitute hazelnuts for the walnuts and chopped candied cherries for the figs.

apple & prune bars

see base recipe page 208

apricot & apple bars
Prepare the basic cookie dough and substitute dried apricots for the prunes.

date & pineapple bars
Prepare the basic cookie dough and substitute dates and pineapple for the prunes and apple.

coconut & cherry bars
Prepare the basic cookie dough and substitute coconut for the rolled oats and cherries for the prunes and apple.

variations

sesame seed cookies

see base recipe page 209

sesame seed & coconut cookies
Prepare the basic cookie dough and substitute ¼ cup flaked coconut for half of the sesame seeds.

sesame & cardamom cookies
Prepare the basic cookie dough and add crushed seeds from 12 cardamom pods.

sesame & ginger cookies
Prepare the basic cookie dough and add ½ teaspoon of ground ginger.

variations

applesauce cookies

see base recipe page 211

applesauce & mint cookies
Prepare the basic cookie dough and add 2 teaspoons freshly
chopped mint.

applesauce & pecan cookies
Prepare the basic cookie dough and add ½ cup (3 oz.) coarsely
chopped pecans.

applesauce & blueberry cookies
Prepare the basic cookie dough and add ¼ cup (2 oz.) dried blueberries.

variations

berry oat bars

see base recipe page 212

pineapple & raisin oat bars
Prepare the basic cookie dough, substituting 1 cup (5 oz.) dried chopped pineapple and ½ cup (3 oz.) raisins for the cherries and berries.

cherry oat bars
Prepare the basic cookie dough, substituting 1 cup (5 oz.) dried sour cherries for the strawberries and blueberries.

pear & ginger oat bars
Prepare the basic cookie dough, substituting 1 cup (3½ oz.) chopped dried pears and 3 tablespoons chopped candied ginger for the cherries and berries.

variations

popcorn puffs

see base recipe page 214

popcorn & fudge puffs
Prepare the basic cookie dough and add 2 tablespoons chopped
fudge pieces.

popcorn & chocolate puffs
Prepare the basic cookie dough and add 2 tablespoons (1 oz.) semisweet
chocolate chips.

popcorn double deckers
Prepare and bake the basic cookie recipe. Take 2 cookies and sandwich
them together with low-fat cream cheese and sugar-free jelly.

cookies for special diets

Just because you have a food allergy or intolerance, it doesn't mean you need to miss out on cookies and bars. Meringue cookies, macaroons, layer bars, and chocolate crunchies are just a few recipes free of wheat, dairy products, gluten, or nuts.

wheat & fruit cookies

see variations page 244

Fruity, nutty, but most importantly, free of added sugar.

½ cup (1 stick) sweet butter
1 egg
Grated zest of 1 orange (2 to 3 tsp.)
1 cup whole-wheat flour
1 tsp. baking powder

Pinch of salt
1 cup flaked coconut
1 cup (5 oz.) chopped dates
½ cup ground pecans

Beat the butter and egg together. Add the orange zest and gradually stir in the whole-wheat flour, baking powder, and salt.

Combine the coconut, dates, and pecans, and stir into the cookie dough.

Divide the dough into 2 and roll into 2 logs about 2½ in. (6.5 cm.) in diameter. Wrap in parchment and refrigerate until firm.

Preheat the oven to 350°F (175°C). Slice the cookies into rounds about ¼ in. (6 mm.) thick. Place on baking sheets and bake for 10 to 12 minutes. Remove from the sheets and cool on wire racks.

Store in an airtight container for 5 to 7 days.

Makes 4 dozen

macaroons

see variations page 245

A simple, wheat-free cookie that is moist and keeps well.

1 cup (5 oz.) ground almonds
1¼ cups superfine sugar
1 tbsp. ground rice
2 egg whites

Preheat the oven to 350°F (175°C). Line baking sheets with rice paper. Mix all the ingredients to a smooth paste.

Pipe small rounds of mixture using a ½-in. (1-cm.) plain nozzle.

Bake for 8 to 10 minutes until golden. Cool on baking sheets and peel off the rice paper to remove.

When completely cool, store in an airtight container for 5 to 7 days.

Makes 2 dozen

almond cookies

see variations page 246

Whether you follow a wheat-free diet or not, you'll love these buttery, crunchy, wheat-free cookies.

½ cup (1 stick) sweet butter
½ cup light brown sugar
1 egg

½ cup rice flour
2 cups crisped rice cereal
2 tbsp. (1 oz.) chopped almonds

Preheat the oven to 350°F (175°C). Beat the butter and sugar together until soft. Add the egg.

Fold in the rice flour, cereal, and almonds.

Roll the dough into balls, place on a large, non-stick baking sheet, and press them with a fork to flatten. Bake for 12 to 15 minutes.

Store in an airtight container for 3 to 4 days.

Makes 1½ dozen

banana cookies

see variations page 247

Big on flavor and very easy to make, these cookies require no added sugar to sweeten them, relying on the natural fruit sugars in the bananas and dates. Made without wheat flour, they are perfect for anyone who wants a healthy, wheat-free snack.

3 ripe bananas
1 cup (5 oz.) pitted dates
2 cups rolled oats

$^1/_3$ cup (80 ml.) oil
1tsp. (5 ml.) vanilla extract

Preheat the oven to 350°F (175°C).

Mash the bananas and chop the dates fine. Mix all the ingredients in a bowl together and put to one side for 15 minutes.

Drop teaspoonfuls onto a non-stick baking sheet and bake for 20 minutes.

Store in an airtight container and eat within 24 hours.

Makes 2$^1/_2$ dozen

coconut wedges

see variations page 248

Dairy-free and sweetened with maple syrup, this coconut oat cookie is a wholesome alternative to mass-produced snack bars.

1¼ cups all-purpose flour
½ tsp. baking powder
½ tsp. baking soda
½ tsp. ground cinnamon
¼ tsp. ground nutmeg
1½ cups flaked coconut

½ cup rolled oats
¾ cup (4 oz.) coarsely chopped pecans
½ cup safflower oil
¾ cup maple syrup
2 eggs
2 tsp. vanilla extract

Preheat the oven to 350°F (175°C). Grease and line a 9 x 13-in. (23 x 33-cm.) pan with parchment.

Sift the flour, baking powder, baking soda, and spices together in a bowl and stir in the coconut, oats, and pecans.

Beat the oil and maple syrup together. Add the eggs and vanilla.

Stir the dry ingredients into the oil and egg mixture. Spread the mixture into the pan. Bake for 12 to 15 minutes. Cut into wedges and transfer to a wire rack to cool. Store in an airtight container for 4 to 5 days.

Makes 2 dozen

dairy-free shortbread

see variations page 249

Crisp, crumbly, and dairy-free, this shortbread is too tasty to resist!

¾ cup margarine
½ cup superfine sugar
2 tsp. vanilla extract

1½ cups all-purpose flour
¼ tsp. salt
2 tsp. granulated sugar

Line a 9-in. (23-cm.) round pan with foil.

Cut the margarine into chunks and gently melt it in a saucepan over a low heat. Remove from the heat, and stir in the superfine sugar and vanilla.

Sift the flour and salt together and stir into the sugar mixture. Spread the mixture evenly into the pan and refrigerate for 2 hours, or until firm.

Preheat the oven to 300°F (150°C). Bake for 55 to 60 minutes. Remove from the oven and sprinkle with granulated sugar. Cut into wedges and cool in a tin.

Store in an airtight container for 5 to 7 days.

Makes 1 dozen

layer bars

see variations page 250

A gluten-free sweet treat that even kids will love.

6 tbsp. (¾ stick) sweet butter
2 cups (7 oz.) gluten-free cookie crumbs
1 cup (5 oz.) semisweet chocolate chips
1 cup (5 oz.) white chocolate chips

1 cup (5 oz.) coarsely chopped pecans
1 cup flaked coconut
1 cup condensed milk

Preheat the oven to 325°F (160°C). Line an 8-in.- (20-cm.-) square pan with parchment.

Melt the butter in a saucepan, remove from the heat, and stir in the cookie crumbs. Press into the pan.

Sprinkle over the chocolate chips, pecans, and coconut. Pour over the condensed milk.

Bake for 30 to 35 minutes. Cool in the pan for at least 1 hour and cut into bars.

Store in an airtight container for 3 to 4 days.

Makes 2½ dozen

berry meringue cookies

see variations page 251

Meringue cookies that can be dressed up as a fancy dessert — simply by sandwiching together with fruit preserve or whipped cream.

3 egg whites
¼ tsp. cream of tartar
½ cup superfine sugar
1 tbsp. cornstarch

1 tsp. white wine vinegar
¼ cup (2 oz.) finely chopped dried blueberries
¼ cup (2 oz.) finely chopped dried cherries

Preheat the oven to 275˚F (140˚C). Line 2 baking sheets with parchment. Whisk the egg whites and cream of tartar. When soft peaks form, add one-third of the sugar. Whisk for another minute, and add another third of the sugar. Whisk for a further minute and add the remaining sugar.

Mix the cornstarch with vinegar and stir into the meringue. Stir in the dried berries.

Drop spoonfuls onto a baking sheet and flatten with the back of the spoon. Bake for 25 to 30 minutes, turn off the oven, and leave inside for an hour. Transfer the parchment sheets to wire racks. Remove when cool.

Store in an airtight container for 2 to 3 days.

Makes 1½ dozen

meringue nut cookies

see variations page 252

Nutty little mouthfuls that are light enough to eat at any time of day.

3 egg whites
¼ tsp. cream of tartar
½ cup superfine sugar
4 tbsp. toasted ground hazelnuts

1 cup (3½ oz.) coarsely chopped
    toasted hazelnuts
Pinch of salt

Preheat the oven to 275°F (140°C). Line 2 baking sheets with parchment.

Whisk the egg whites and cream of tartar. When soft peaks form add one-third of the sugar. Whisk for a further minute, then add another third of the sugar. Whisk for another minute and add the remaining sugar.

Fold the hazelnuts and salt into the meringue.

Drop spoonfuls onto a baking sheet and bake for 25 to 30 minutes. Turn off the oven and leave inside for 1 hour. Transfer the parchment sheets to wire racks. Remove when cool.

Store in an airtight container for 4 to 5 days.

Makes 2 dozen

bittersweet chocolate crunchies

see variations page 253

These are everyone's favorite refrigerator cookie — and especially easy to make with kids.

7 oz. bittersweet chocolate
¼ cup (½ stick) sweet butter
5 tbsp. corn syrup
3 cups crisped rice cereal

Line 2 baking sheets with parchment.

Melt the chocolate and butter together in a heatproof bowl over a saucepan of simmering water, or in the microwave.

Stir in the corn syrup and crisped rice cereal. Drop spoonfuls of the mixture onto the baking sheets and refrigerate for about 45 minutes, until set.

Store in an airtight container in the fridge for 5 to 7 days.

Makes 2 dozen

variations

wheat & fruit cookies

see base recipe page 229

date & walnut cookies
Prepare the basic cookie dough and substitute walnuts for the pecans.

fig & raisin cookies
Prepare the basic cookie dough and substitute ½ cup (3 oz.) raisins and ½ cup (3 oz.) chopped figs for the dates.

variations

macaroons

see base recipe page 231

pistachio macaroons
Prepare the basic cookie dough and substitute ground pistachios for half
the ground almonds. Top each piped macaroon with a pistachio.

walnut macaroons
Prepare the basic cookie dough and substitute ground walnuts for half the
ground almonds. Top each piped macaroon with a walnut half.

hazelnut macaroons
Prepare the basic cookie dough and substitute ground hazelnuts for half the
ground almonds. Top each piped macaroon with a hazelnut.

variations

almond cookies

see base recipe page 232

almond & cherry cookies
Prepare the basic cookie dough and add ¼ cup (2 oz.) dried cherries.

pine nut & lemon cookies
Prepare the basic cookie dough, substituting pine nuts for the almonds.

almond & cranberry cookies
Prepare the basic cookie dough and add ¼ cup (2 oz.) dried cranberries.

variations

banana cookies

see base recipe page 233

banana & rum cookies
Prepare the basic cookie dough and add 2 tablespoons dark rum.

spiced banana cookies
Prepare the basic cookie dough, and add ½ teaspoon ground cinnamon and ¼ teaspoon ground ginger.

banana & coconut cookies
Prepare the basic cookie dough, substituting flaked coconut for ¼ cup of the rolled oats.

variations

coconut wedges

see base recipe page 234

pineapple coconut wedges
Prepare the basic cookie dough and substitute ½ cup (3 oz.) chopped dried pineapple for the pecans.

cherry coconut wedges
Prepare the basic cookie dough and substitute ½ cup (3 oz.) dried cherries for the pecans.

apricot coconut wedges
Prepare the basic cookie dough and substitute ½ cup (3 oz.) chopped dried apricots for the pecans.

dairy-free shortbread

see base recipe page 236

brown sugar shortbread
Prepare the basic cookie dough and substitute unrefined dark brown sugar
for half of the superfine sugar.

spiced pecan shortbread
Prepare the basic cookie dough, decreasing the flour to 1¼ cups. Process
½ cup (2 oz.) whole toasted pecans until they are finely ground and then
add the nuts to the flour with ½ teaspoon ground cinnamon and ¼ teaspoon
ground nutmeg.

cherry shortbread
Prepare the basic cookie dough, and add 1 cup (5 oz.) chopped candied red
cherries to the mixture with the flour.

variations

layer bars

see base recipe page 237

butterscotch layer bar
Prepare the basic cookie dough and substitute butterscotch chips for
the white chocolate chips.

peanut layer bars
Prepare the basic cookie dough and substitute peanut butter pieces for
the white chocolate chips and peanuts for the pecans.

raisin layer bar
Prepare the basic cookie dough and substitute raisins for the white
chocolate chips.

variations

berry meringue cookies

see base recipe page 239

fresh berry meringues
Prepare the basic cookie dough and substitute ½ cup (3 oz.) fresh blueberries for the dried berries. You will need to eat these meringues on the day they are made.

cranberry meringues
Prepare the basic cookie dough and substitute cranberries and the grated zest of one orange (1 to 2 teaspoons) for the blueberries and cherries.

blueberry & lemon meringues
Prepare the basic cookie dough, but substitute more dried blueberries for the dried cherries. Add the grated zest of one lemon (1 to 2 teaspoons).

variations

meringue nut cookies

see base recipe page 240

macadamia meringue nut cookies
Prepare the basic cookie dough and substitute macadamia nuts for the hazelnuts.

pecan & cinnamon meringue nut cookies
Prepare the basic cookie dough and substitute pecans for hazelnuts. Add ½ teaspoon ground cinnamon to the sugar.

brazil nut meringue cookies
Prepare the basic cookie dough and substitute brazil nuts for the hazelnuts. Replace half the superfine sugar with unrefined light brown sugar.

variations

bittersweet chocolate crunchies

see base recipe page 243

chocolate raisin crunchies
Prepare the basic cookie dough and add ½ cup (3 oz.) raisins to the mixture.

chocolate chip & pecan crunchies
Prepare the basic cookie dough and add ½ cup (3 oz.) white chocolate chips
and ½ cup (3 oz.) coarsely chopped pecans to the mixture.

chocolate cherry crunchies
Prepare the basic cookie dough and add ½ cup (3 oz.) chopped red candied
cherries to the mixture.

cookie bars

Rather than being shaped into individual cookies, these classic cookies are baked in a tray and then sliced into wedges, squares, or fingers. Brownies, fruit and nut slices, millionaire's shortbread, and turtle bars — cookie bars have become so popular they deserve a chapter of their own.

lemon bars

see variations page 273

These sharp-tasting little bars are sure to become a fast favorite with the family.

for the crust

½ cup (1 stick) sweet butter
¼ cup superfine sugar
1 tsp. vanilla extract
1 cup all-purpose flour
Pinch of salt

for the topping

¼ cup superfine sugar
2 tbsp. all-purpose flour
2 eggs
½ cup lemon curd
⅓ cup fresh lemon juice
2 tbsp. confectioners' sugar to dust

Preheat the oven to 350°F (175°C). Line an 8-in.- (20-cm.-) square pan with foil. Cut the butter into chunks and melt in a saucepan over a gentle heat. Remove from the heat and stir in the sugar and vanilla. Then stir in the sifted flour and salt. Press the dough into the bottom of the pan. Bake for 30 minutes until the crust is golden. Remove from the oven and reduce the temperature to 300°F (150°C).

While the crust is baking, stir together the sugar and flour for the topping in a large bowl. Whisk in the eggs. Stir in the lemon curd and lemon juice. When the crust is cooked, pour the filling over the base and bake for 20 minutes or until lightly set. Cool in a pan then transfer the foil to a cutting board. Cut into squares and store in an airtight container for 2 to 3 days. Before serving, dust with confectioners' sugar.

Makes 2½ dozen

brownies

see variations page 274

Everyone loves brownies and everyone has a favorite recipe. This is mine, adapted from a recipe given to me by my friend, a pastry chef, who used to make brownies in Joe Allen Restaurant in London, England.

½ cup (1 stick) sweet butter
4 oz. unsweetened chocolate
4 oz. bittersweet chocolate
1 cup unrefined light brown sugar
Pinch of salt

1 tsp. vanilla extract
2 eggs
¼ cup all-purpose flour
1 cup (3½ oz.) coarsely chopped pecans

Preheat the oven to 325°F (160°C). Line the base and sides of an 8-in.- (20-cm.-) square pan with parchment.

Melt the butter and chocolate in a heatproof bowl over a saucepan of simmering water or in the microwave on a low heat. Once melted, stir to blend the butter and chocolate together, then add the sugar, salt, and vanilla. Beat in the eggs one at a time then beat in the flour and half the pecans. When the batter is smooth, pour into the pan, sprinkle over the remaining pecans, and bake for 35 to 40 minutes.

Cool in the pan for at least 20 minutes then lift the parchment and transfer the brownies to a chopping board. Cut into squares and store in an airtight container for 3 to 4 days.

Makes 2½ dozen

nut brittle squares

see variations page 275

Crunchy fruit and nut bites to accompany the froth on your morning cappuccino.

for the crust

½ cup (1 stick) sweet butter
1⅓ cups all-purpose flour
¼ tsp. salt
¼ cup superfine sugar
1 egg

for the topping

1¼ cups (2½ sticks) sweet butter
½ cup clear honey
1½ cups superfine sugar
⅓ cup heavy cream
1 cup (3½ oz.) coarsely chopped candied fruit
1 cup (3½ oz.) coarsely chopped hazelnuts
1 cup (3½ oz.) coarsely chopped walnuts

Preheat the oven to 350°F (175°C). Line a 9 x 13-in. (23 x 33-cm.) pan with parchment. Cut the butter into chunks and put into the food processor with the flour, salt, and sugar. Process until the mixture resembles breadcrumbs, then add the egg and process until the mixture comes together. Press into the base of the pan. Bake for 15 to 20 minutes until golden.

Put the butter, honey, and sugar in a heavy saucepan and cook over a moderate heat for 15 to 20 minutes, stirring frequently. Remove from the heat and stir in the cream, fruit, and nuts. Pour onto the crust, level the surface, put the pan on a baking sheet and bake for 15 to 20 minutes. Remove from the oven and allow to cool before cutting into squares. Store in an airtight container for 5 to 7 days.

Makes 2½ dozen

toffee bars

see variations page 276

Buttery shortbread and lashings of chocolate studded with nuts and fudge pieces make these a favorite with the kids.

For the crust

½ cup (1 stick) sweet butter
½ cup light brown sugar
1 tsp. vanilla extract
1 cup all-purpose flour
Pinch of salt

For the topping

6 oz. semisweet chocolate, chopped into small pieces
½ cup (2 oz.) chopped fudge pieces
½ cup (2 oz.) chopped toasted almonds

Preheat the oven to 350°F (175°C). Line the base and sides of an 8-in.- (20-cm.-) square pan with foil.

Cut the butter into chunks and melt in a saucepan over a gentle heat. Remove from the heat and stir in the sugar and vanilla. Then stir in the sifted flour and salt. Press the dough into the bottom of the pan.

Bake for 20 to 25 minutes until golden. Remove from the oven and sprinkle with chocolate, fudge pieces, and almonds and return to the oven for 2 to 3 minutes to melt the chocolate. Allow to cool in the pan, then lift the foil and transfer to a chopping board. Cut into bars. Store in an airtight container for 5 to 7 days.

Makes 2½ dozen

honey nut squares

see variations page 277

These chewy honey squares are packed full with crunchy nuts surrounded by soft toffee.

for the crust

½ cup (1 stick) sweet butter
1⅓ cups all-purpose flour
¼ tsp. salt
¼ cup superfine sugar
1 egg

for the topping

1½ cups (8 oz.) lightly toasted macadamia nuts
¾ cup superfine sugar
¼ cup honey
½ cup (1 stick) sweet butter
⅔ cup heavy cream

Preheat the oven to 350°F (175°C). Line a 9 x 13-in. (23 x 33-cm.) pan with parchment. Put the butter in a food processor with the flour, salt, and sugar. Process until the mixture resembles breadcrumbs, then add the egg and process until it comes together. Press into the base of the pan. Bake for 15 to 20 minutes until golden.

Process the macadamia nuts in a food processor for 30 seconds. Put the sugar, honey, butter, and cream into a heavy saucepan and using a candy thermometer, cook to medium ball stage 240°F (118°C). Put the nuts on a baking sheet and warm in the oven for a few minutes. Remove the thermometer and place it in a jug of boiling water. Take the pan off the heat and quickly stir in the warmed nuts. Pour the mixture onto the crust and bake for 5 minutes. Remove from the oven and allow to set for about 2 hours. Cut into squares and store in an airtight container for 5 to 7 days.

Makes 2 dozen

turtle bars

see variations page 278

If you have not tried turtle bars — you need to! This wonderful combination of American flavors is divine — chewy caramel, pecans, and chocolate on a shortbread base.

for the crust

¾ cup (1½ sticks) sweet butter
⅓ cup superfine sugar
1 tsp. vanilla extract
2 cups all-purpose flour
Pinch of salt
2 cups (7 oz.) pecan halves

for the topping

½ cup (1 stick) sweet butter
¾ cup light brown sugar
5 oz. semisweet chocolate chips

Preheat the oven to 350°F (175°C). Line a 9 x 13-in. (23 x 33-cm.) pan with foil. Cut the butter into chunks and melt in a saucepan over a gentle heat. Remove from the heat and stir in the sugar and vanilla. Stir in the sifted flour and salt. Press the dough into the bottom of the pan. Bake for 10 minutes then scatter over the pecans and bake for 10 minutes more until the crust is golden. Remove from the oven.

Melt the butter and stir in the sugar. Bring the mixture to a boil and boil for 1 minute. Pour the hot butter mixture over the crust. Bake for 10 minutes then remove from the oven and sprinkle over the chocolate chips. Cool in the pan. Lift the foil and transfer to a chopping board. Cut into bars. Store in an airtight container for 5 to 7 days.

Makes 2 dozen

chewy almond cherry bars

see variations page 279

Super little snack bars that are light, tasty, and not too sweet.

1 cup (5 oz.) whole almonds	½ cup (1 stick) sweet butter
¾ cup all-purpose flour	¾ cup light brown sugar
½ tsp. baking powder	1 egg
Pinch of salt	½ cup (3 oz.) dried cherries

Preheat the oven to 350°F (175°C). Line the base and sides of an 8-in.- (20-cm.-) square pan with parchment.

Put the almonds in a food processor and process until they are finely ground. Then add the flour, baking powder, and salt, and process to mix.

Cut the butter into chunks and melt in a saucepan over a gentle heat. Remove from the heat and stir in the sugar and egg. Then stir in the dry ingredients and cherries. Spread the batter into the pan and bake for 20 to 25 minutes until golden. Cool in the pan. Lift the parchment and transfer to a chopping board. Cut into bars.

Store in an airtight container for 5 to 7 days.

Makes 2½ dozen

fruit & nut slices

see variations page 280

These tasty bars make an irresistible mid-morning snack.

⅓ cup all-purpose flour	2 cups (7 oz.) pecan pieces
Pinch of baking powder	2 cups (10 oz.) pitted and chopped dates
Pinch of baking soda	1 cup (5 oz.) coarsely chopped dried apricots
Pinch of salt	1 egg
¼ cup light brown sugar	1 tsp. vanilla extract

Preheat the oven to 350°F (175°C). Line the base and sides of an 8-in.- (20-cm.-) square pan with parchment.

Sift the flour, baking powder, baking soda, and salt together in a bowl. Add the sugar and fruits and coat them in the flour. In a separate bowl, beat the egg and vanilla until pale and thick, then add to the fruit and flour mix. Mix with your hands until all the fruit is evenly coated in batter. Spread the mixture into the pan and bake for 35 to 40 minutes until golden brown. Lift the parchment and transfer to a chopping board. Cut into slices.

Store in an airtight container for 5 to 7 days.

Makes 2½ dozen

cream cheese cookie slices

see variations page 281

Chocolate and cream cheese combine to great effect in these cookie slices.

¾ cup (1½ sticks) sweet butter
7 oz. bittersweet chocolate
2 cups superfine sugar
4 eggs

2 tsp. vanilla extract
2 cups all-purpose flour
1 cup (9 oz.) cream cheese
5 oz. coarsely chopped semisweet chocolate

Preheat the oven to 350°F (175°C). Line a 9 x 13-in. (23 x 33-cm.) pan with parchment.

Melt the butter and bittersweet chocolate in a heatproof bowl over a saucepan of simmering water or in the microwave on low. Once melted, stir to blend the butter and chocolate together, then add 1½ cups of sugar, the eggs, and the vanilla. Stir in the flour and spread the batter into the pan.

Beat the cream cheese and remaining sugar and stir in the semisweet chocolate chunks. Drop spoonfuls over chocolate batter and swirl the two batters together with a knife to give a marbled effect. Bake for 30 to 35 minutes until lightly set. Cool completely in the pan. Lift the parchment and transfer to a chopping board. Cut into bars.

Store in an airtight container and refrigerate for 3 to 4 days.

Makes 2 dozen

blondies

see variations page 282

As their name suggests, blondies are golden in color. Light brown sugar gives the best result. This version, packed full with nuts and chocolate chips, is fantastic.

1 cup all-purpose flour
¾ tsp. baking powder
Pinch of salt
½ cup (1 stick) sweet butter
1 cup light brown sugar

1 egg
1 tsp. vanilla extract
¾ cup (3 oz.) coarsely chopped walnuts
¾ cup (4 oz.) semisweet chocolate chips

Preheat the oven to 350°F (175°C). Line the base and sides of an 8-in.- (20-cm.-) square pan with parchment.

Sift the flour, baking powder, and salt together in a bowl. Cut the butter into chunks and melt in a saucepan over a gentle heat. Remove from the heat and stir in the brown sugar. Beat in the egg and vanilla, then stir in the flour mixture, walnuts, and chocolate chips. Bake for 20 to 25 minutes until golden. Remove from the oven and allow to cool in the pan. Lift the parchment and transfer the blondies to a chopping board.

Cut into squares and store in an airtight container for 2 to 3 days.

Makes 2 dozen

tropical bars

see variations page 283

Eating these tangy, fruity bars is a full-blown Calypso experience you must not miss out on — once tasted, never forgotten.

½ cup (1 stick) sweet butter
1 cup (8 oz.) peanut butter
½ cup light brown sugar
½ cup (3 oz.) chopped dates

¼ cup (2 oz.) chopped dried mango
¼ cup (2 oz.) chopped dried pineapple
1 tbsp. flaked coconut
2½ cups crisped rice cereal

Line an 8-in.- (20-cm.-) square pan with parchment.

Cut the butter into chunks and melt in a saucepan over a gentle heat. Stir in the peanut butter and then the sugar, and stir to combine.

Remove from the heat and add the dates, dried mango, and pineapple. Stir in the coconut and rice cereal. Press the mixture into the pan and refrigerate until firm. Remove from pan and cut into bars.

Store in an airtight container in the fridge for 5 to 7 days.

Makes 2½ dozen

white chocolate fudge bars

see variations page 284

Wonderfully moist with a touch of vanilla, these white chocolate fudge bars are
a change from the usual chocolate bars.

1½ cups all-purpose flour
½ tsp. baking soda
½ cup (1 stick) sweet butter
3 oz. white chocolate
2 eggs

2 cups superfine sugar
2 tsp. vanilla extract
½ cup (2 oz.) chopped toasted hazelnuts
½ cup (3 oz.) white chocolate chips

Preheat the oven to 350°F (175°C). Line a 9 x 13-in.- (23 x 33-cm.-) deep pan with parchment.
Sift the flour and baking soda together in a bowl. Melt the butter and white chocolate in
a heatproof bowl over a saucepan of simmering water, or in the microwave on a low heat.

In a separate bowl, beat the eggs until foamy, then beat in the sugar until well-blended. Stir
in the melted chocolate, butter, and vanilla.

Add the dry ingredients and spoon into the pan. Level the surface and sprinkle with the
chocolate chips. Place the pan on a baking sheet and bake for 25 to 30 minutes. Remove
from the oven, allow to cool in the tray for 10 minutes, then invert onto parchment on
a wire tray and cool for 30 minutes. Invert onto chopping board and cut into bars. When
completely cool, store in an airtight container for 5 to 7 days.

Makes 2 dozen

millionaire's shortbread

see variations page 285

Millionaire's shortbread is appropriately named, given that it is rich and extravagant!

1¼ cups all-purpose flour
½ cup confectioners' sugar
1½ cups (3 sticks) sweet butter
5 tbsp. corn syrup

One 14-oz. can condensed milk
1 tsp. vanilla extract
7 oz. semisweet chocolate
1 tbsp. safflower oil

Preheat the oven to 350°F (175°C). Line the base of a 9 x 13-in. (23 x 33-cm.) pan with foil.

Sift the flour and confectioners' sugar together in a bowl, and then cut in 1 cup (2 sticks) butter until the mixture starts to come together. Press the dough into the base of the pan. Bake for 15 to 20 minutes until golden.

For the caramel, melt the remaining butter in the microwave and then stir in the corn syrup and condensed milk. Microwave on high for 8 to 9 minutes, stirring every 1 to 2 minutes. Stir in the vanilla and spread over the warm shortbread. Refrigerate for about 2 hours until firm. Melt the chocolate in a heatproof bowl over a saucepan of simmering water or in the microwave on a low heat, then stir in the safflower oil. Spread over the caramel and refrigerate for 15 minutes, then cut into squares.

When completely cool, store in an airtight container for 5 to 7 days.

Makes 2½ dozen

variations

lemon bars

see base recipe page 255

hazelnut crusted lemon bars
Prepare the basic cookie dough, putting the sugar, salt, and flour less 3 tablespoons in a food processor with ¼ cup (1 oz.) toasted skinned hazelnuts. Grind the mixture to a fine powder, then add the melted butter. Press into the pan and bake. Prepare the crust and topping in the base recipe.

apricot & lemon bars
Prepare the basic cookie dough, substituting apricot preserve for the lemon curd.

lemon & lime bars
Prepare the basic cookie dough, substituting lime juice for the lemon juice.

variations

brownies

see base recipe page 257

chocolate chip brownies
Prepare the basic cookie dough and substitute ½ cup (3 oz.) semisweet chocolate chips for the pecans.

cream cheese brownies
Prepare the basic cookie dough, then put a third of the batter into a separate bowl. Add ½ cup (4½ oz.) cream cheese and mix to incorporate. Pour the chocolate brownie batter into the pan and swirl through the cream cheese batter to give a marbled effect.

mocha brownies
Prepare the basic cookie dough and add ½ cup (3 oz.) semisweet chocolate chips and 2 tablespoons strong instant coffee powder to the batter.

variations

nut brittle squares

see base recipe page 258

cherry nut brittle squares
Prepare the basic cookie dough, and substitute ¼ cup (2 oz.) dried cherries
and ¼ cup (2 oz.) chopped candied cherries for the candied fruit.

pecan & chocolate nut brittle squares
Prepare the basic cookie dough, and substitute pecans for the walnuts and
¼ cup (2 oz.) chopped candied cherries and ¼ cup (2 oz.) semisweet chocolate
chips for the candied fruit.

almond & ginger nut brittle squares
Prepare the basic cookie dough, and substitute flaked almonds for the
walnuts, and ¼ cup (2 oz.) chopped candied ginger for the candied fruit.

variations

toffee bars

see base recipe page 259

cherry toffee bars
Prepare the basic cookie dough and substitute chopped red candied cherries for the fudge pieces.

hazelnut toffee bars
Prepare the basic cookie dough and substitute skinned chopped toasted hazelnuts for the almonds.

white chocolate chip toffee bars
Prepare the basic cookie dough and add ¼ cup (2 oz.) white chocolate chips to the topping.

variations

honey nut squares

see base recipe page 260

pecan honey nut squares
Prepare the basic cookie dough, and substitute pecans for the macadamia nuts. As pecans are softer than macadamias, process them for only about 20 seconds in the food processor.

walnut, honey, & cherry squares
Prepare the basic cookie dough, substituting walnuts for the macadamia nuts and add ½ cup (3 oz.) chopped red candied cherries with the nuts.

almond & ginger honey nut squares
Prepare the basic cookie dough, substituting whole skinned almonds for the macadamia nuts, and add 2 tablespoons chopped candied ginger with the nuts.

variations

turtle bars

see base recipe page 263

double chocolate nut turtle bars
Prepare the basic cookie dough, substituting skinned hazelnuts for half the pecans and white chocolate chips for half the semisweet chocolate.

fudge turtle bars
Prepare the basic cookie dough and add ¼ cup (2 oz.) chopped fudge pieces to the hot topping before the chocolate chips.

marshmallow turtle bars
Prepare the basic cookie dough and add ½ cup (2 oz.) miniature marshmallows to the hot topping before the chocolate chips.

chewy almond cherry bars

see base recipe page 264

almond & date bars
Prepare the basic cookie dough and substitute ½ cup (3 oz.) chopped dates for the cherries.

cranberry, orange & almond bars
Prepare the basic cookie dough and substitute ½ cup (3 oz.) dried cranberries for the cherries, and add the grated zest of 1 orange (2 to 3 teaspoons).

hazelnut pear bars
Prepare the basic cookie dough and substitute hazelnuts for the almonds and chopped dried pear for the cherries.

variations

fruit & nut slices

see base recipe page 265

blueberry & walnut slices
Prepare the basic cookie dough and substitute walnuts for the pecans and dried blueberries for the dates.

pear & almond slices
Prepare the basic cookie dough and substitute coarsely chopped almonds for the pecans and chopped dried pears for the apricots.

pineapple & apricot slices
Prepare the basic cookie dough and substitute ½ cup (3 oz.) chopped dried pineapple for ½ cup (3 oz.) of the dates.

variations

cream cheese cookie slices

see base recipe page 266

chocolate orange cream cheese cookie slices
Prepare the basic cookie dough and add the grated zest of 1 orange
(2 to 3 teaspoons) to the chocolate batter.

fudge nut cream cheese cookie slices
Prepare the basic cookie dough and add ½ cup (3 oz.) coarsely chopped
pecans to the chocolate batter and ½ cup (3 oz.) chopped fudge pieces
to the cream cheese batter.

mocha cream cheese cookie slices
Prepare the basic cookie dough and add 2 tablespoons instant coffee powder
to the cream cheese batter before swirling it in the chocolate batter.

variations

blondies

see base recipe page 268

butterscotch blondies
Prepare the basic cookie dough and substitute ¼ cup (2 oz.) butterscotch chips for ¼ cup (1 oz.) walnuts.

pecan & white chocolate chip blondies
Prepare the basic cookie dough and substitute pecans for the walnuts and white chocolate chips for the semisweet chocolate chips.

double chocolate chip blondies
Prepare the basic cookie dough and substitute ¼ cup (2 oz.) white chocolate chips for half the walnuts.

tropical bars

see base recipe page 269

date & cherry bars
Prepare the basic cookie dough and substitute chopped red candied cherries for the dried mango and pineapple.

chocolate & coconut bars
Prepare the basic cookie dough and substitute ½ cup (3 oz.) semisweet chocolate chips for the dried mango and pineapple.

ginger tropical bars
Prepare the basic cookie dough and add 2 tablespoons chopped candied ginger.

variations

white chocolate fudge bars

see base recipe page 271

white chocolate butterscotch bars
Prepare the basic cookie dough and substitute light brown sugar for the superfine sugar and butterscotch chips for the white chocolate chips.

double chocolate fudge bars
Prepare the basic cookie dough and substitute bittersweet chocolate for the white chocolate.

chocolate cherry fudge bars
Prepare the basic cookie dough and substitute bittersweet chocolate for the white chocolate, and add ½ cup (3 oz.) chopped red candied cherries.

variations

millionaire's shortbread

see base recipe page 272

chocolate chip millionaire's shortbread
Prepare the basic cookie dough and sprinkle ¼ cup (2 oz.) bittersweet
chocolate chips over the shortbread base before spreading the caramel
on top.

chocolate orange millionaire's shortbread
Prepare the basic cookie dough, adding the grated zest of 1 orange
(2 to 3 teaspoons) to the chocolate before spreading it over the
firm caramel.

nut crusted millionaire's shortbread
Prepare the basic cookie dough but substitute ¼ cup (1½ oz.) toasted
ground hazelnuts for ¼ cup flour.

dessert cookies

Delicate wafer-thin cookies such as langue de chat and brandy snaps can transform a simple bowl of ice cream into a sophisticated dessert. This chapter is dedicated to your after-dinner guests, with ideas of what to serve with coffee and wine, and how to impress with home-made macaroons and amaretti.

langue de chat

see variations page 310

Langue de chat, or "cat's tongue," is a wafer-thin delicate biscuit that can be served with ice cream sundaes or individual mousse desserts.

¼ cup (½ stick) sweet butter
¼ cup confectioners' sugar, sifted
2 egg whites
⅓ cup plus 2 tbsp. all-purpose flour, sifted

Preheat the oven to 400°F (200°C). Grease 2 baking sheets.

Beat the butter and sugar together until light and fluffy. Add the egg whites and mix to incorporate. Stir in the flour.

Pipe the mixture using a piping bag and a ¼-in. (6-mm.) plain nozzle, making 1½-in. (4-cm.) lengths 1½ in. (4 cm.) apart. Bake for 4 to 5 minutes until golden. Remove from the oven and transfer to a baking sheet.

When cool, store in an airtight container for 5 to 7 days.

Makes 3 dozen

french macaroons

see variations page 311

These light macaroons can be found throughout the pâtisseries of Paris.

3 cups confectioners' sugar, sifted
2¼ scant cups ground almonds
7 egg whites

A couple of drops pink food color
¼ tsp. cream of tartar
¼ cup strawberry fruit preserve

Preheat the oven to 400°F (200°C). Line 2 baking sheets with parchment. Mix the sugar and 2 cups together with the almonds. Beat in 3 of the egg whites and enough food color to turn the mixture light pink.

Beat the remaining 4 egg whites with the cream of tartar until soft peaks form. Add one-third of the remaining sugar. Beat for 1 to 2 minutes until the egg whites are stiff, and add another third of the sugar. Beat for one minute and add the remaining sugar. Beat until the meringue is glossy. Add a quarter of the meringue to the dry ingredients, and blend — do not try to fold all the meringue in at this stage. Add another quarter of the meringue, and lift the mixture through with a balloon whisk. Add the remaining meringue in the same way.

Pipe the mixture using a piping bag and ½-in. (1-cm.) nozzle, making 1-in. (2.5-cm.) bulbs, 1 in. (2.5 cm.) apart on the baking sheets. Bake for 5 to 6 minutes. Allow to cool and remove from the parchment. Spread the bases of half the macaroons with strawberry fruit preserve and sandwich with the remaining halves. Store in an airtight container for 5 to 7 days.

Makes 2 dozen

brandy snaps

see variations page 312

Lacy in appearance, these spicy cookies are divine either filled with cream or simply served plain with ice cream.

½ cup (1 stick) sweet butter
½ cup plus 1 tbsp. superfine sugar
4 tbsp. corn syrup

¾ cup all-purpose flour
1 tsp. ground ginger
2 tsp. brandy

Preheat the oven to 350°F (175°C). Line 2 baking sheets with parchment.

Cut the butter into chunks and melt in a saucepan over a gentle heat. Add the sugar and corn syrup, and stir until the sugar dissolves. Remove from the heat.

Sift the flour and ginger together and stir into the butter mixture with the brandy.

Drop spoonfuls onto the baking sheets 3 to 4 in. (8 to 10 cm.) apart. Bake for 5 to 6 minutes until golden. Remove the brandy snaps one at a time, and roll them around the handle of a wooden spoon. Twist gently to lift them off the handle. Cool on a wire rack.

Store unfilled in an airtight container for 5 to 7 days.

Makes 2 dozen

vanilla crescents

see variations page 313

Delicate crumbly little cookies that can be served plain, or half-dipped in melted chocolate and used to accompany other desserts.

1 cup all-purpose flour, sifted	½ cup ground almonds
½ cup (1 stick) sweet butter	2 tbsp. superfine sugar
2 tsp. vanilla extract	1 cup confectioners' sugar

Preheat the oven to 350°F (175°C). Line 2 baking sheets with parchment.

Cut the butter into the flour until the mixture resembles fine breadcrumbs. Add vanilla and stir in the ground almonds and sugar. Work the mixture with your hands until it forms a soft dough.

Roll small pieces of dough into lengths about ½-in. (1-cm.) thick and 2-in. (5-cm.) long, and shape into crescents. Bake for 20 minutes, until pale golden in color.

Remove from the baking sheets, and cool on wire racks. Roll each of the crescents in confectioners' sugar.

Store in an airtight container for 5 to 7 days.

Makes 1½ dozen

sugared sablé

see variations page 314

Serve these delicate buttery cookies with soft textured desserts, or enjoy them on their own with a glass of dessert wine.

3 cups all-purpose flour
1¼ cups confectioners' sugar
1¼ cups (2¼ sticks) sweet butter

2 tsp. vanilla extract
1 egg white
2 tbsp. granulated sugar

Grease and flour 2 baking sheets. Sift the flour and confectioners' sugar together, and cut in the butter.

When the mixture starts to come together, add vanilla extract. Knead the dough lightly until smooth. Divide the dough into 4, and roll into 4 1½-in.- (4-cm.-) wide logs. Wrap in parchment and refrigerate until firm.

Preheat the oven to 375°F (190°C). Brush each log with egg white and roll in the granulated sugar. Cut into ¼-in. (6-mm.) thick slices. Place the cookie slices on the baking sheets and bake for 8 to 10 minutes. Cool on a wire rack.

Store in an airtight container for 5 to 7 days.

Makes 3½ dozen

brittle cookies

see variations page 315

Enjoy these cookies with chocolate- and coffee-flavored desserts.

¼ cup (½ stick) sweet butter
⅓ cup light brown sugar
2 tbsp. corn syrup
1 tbsp. instant coffee powder

Grated zest of 1 orange (2 to 3 tsp.)
½ cup all-purpose flour
½ cup (3 oz.) toasted flaked hazelnuts

Preheat the oven to 350°F (175°C). Line 2 baking sheets with parchment.

Cut the butter into chunks and place in a large saucepan with the sugar and corn syrup. Cook over a gentle heat, stirring until the sugar has dissolved.

Add the instant coffee and orange zest, and stir until the coffee powder has dissolved. Remove from the heat and stir in the flour. Drop teaspoonfuls onto baking sheets 2 in. (5 cm.) apart and sprinkle with nuts. Bake for 10 to 12 minutes.

Remove from the oven and allow to cool on sheets for 1 to 2 minutes before transferring to wire racks to cool.

When completely cool, store in an airtight container for 5 to 7 days.

Makes 2 dozen

florentines

see variations page 316

These delectable nutty cookies are thought to have originated in Florence, Italy.

¾ cup (4 oz.) slivered almonds
2 tbsp. (1 oz.) chopped red candied cherries
2 tbsp. (1 oz.) chopped candied lemon and
    orange peel
⅓ cup plus 2 tbsp. (¾ stick) butter

½ cup superfine sugar
2 tbsp. honey
2 tbsp. heavy cream
4 oz. semisweet chocolate, chopped
2 tsp. safflower oil

Preheat the oven to 350°F (175°C). Line 2 baking sheets with parchment. Mix the almonds, cherries, and candied peel in a bowl and put to one side. Cut the butter into chunks and place in a large saucepan with the sugar and honey. Bring to a boil, stirring occasionally until the mixture thickens slightly. Remove from the heat and stir in the fruit and nuts. Stir in the cream. Allow the mixture to stand for 1 to 2 minutes.

Drop spoonfuls of the dough onto the baking sheets 2 in. (5 cm.) apart. Flatten with the back of a fork dipped in water. Bake for 5 to 7 minutes until golden. Remove from the oven. Using a round cookie cutter, pull the florentines back into shape before they set. Allow to cool completely before removing from the sheet. Melt the chocolate in a heatproof bowl over a saucepan of simmering water, and stir in the oil. Dip the undersides of the florentines in chocolate, and place them on the parchment. Refrigerate for 5 minutes to set the chocolate.

Once set, store the cookies in an airtight container for 5 to 7 days.

Makes 2 dozen

boules de neige

see variations page 317

Boules de neige, or "coconut snowballs," are crunchy dessert accompaniments.

3 egg whites
¼ tsp. cream of tartar
½ cup superfine sugar

1 cup flaked coconut
Pinch of salt
3 tbsp. strawberry fruit preserve

Preheat the oven to 350°F (175°C). Line 2 baking sheets with parchment.

Whisk the egg whites and cream of tartar. When soft peaks form, add one-third of the sugar. Whisk for a minute and add another third of the sugar. Whisk for a further minute, and add the rest of the sugar. Fold the coconut and salt into the meringue.

Use a piping bag and a ½-in. (1-cm.) nozzle to pipe small rounds ½ in. (1 cm.) in diameter onto a baking sheet. Bake for 8 to 10 minutes. Transfer the parchment sheets to wire racks. Remove meringues when cool.

Spread the bases of half the boules de neige with fruit preserve and sandwich with the remaining cookie halves. Serve immediately.

Store the unfilled cookies in an airtight container for 5 to 7 days.

Makes 1½ dozen

orange almond tuiles

see variations page 318

These crispy almond cookies are shaped like continental tiles — hence their name, which means "tile" in French.

⅔ cup all-purpose flour
1 cup confectioners' sugar
1 cup (5 oz.) slivered almonds
1 egg

2 egg whites
Grated zest of 1 orange (2 to 3 tsp.)
3 tbsp. sweet butter, melted

Preheat the oven to 400°F (200°C). Grease 2 baking sheets with butter.

Sift the flour and confectioners' sugar together and stir in the almonds. Add the egg and egg whites to the dry ingredients, and stir to combine. Add the orange zest and melted butter.

Spoon walnut-sized amounts of the dough onto the sheets and flatten with the back of a fork dipped in cold water. In order to allow them enough time to assume a shape, bake one sheet at a time. Bake for 4 to 5 minutes until pale with a darker golden brown edge. Remove from the oven and shape over a rolling pin.

When completely cool, store in an airtight container for 3 to 4 days, or in the freezer for 3 to 4 weeks.

Makes 3 dozen

almond & lemon cantucci

see variations page 319

Best enjoyed with a glass of after-dinner wine.

2 eggs
¾ cup superfine sugar
1 cup (5 oz.) whole almonds

Grated zest of 1 lemon (2 to 3 tsp.)
1⅔ cups all-purpose flour

Preheat the oven to 400°F (200°C). Grease and flour 2 baking sheets.

Beat the eggs and sugar together in a large bowl. Add the nuts and lemon zest and mix into the flour to form a stiff paste. Divide the dough in half and shape into 2 flat loaves about 10 in. (25 cm.) long and 2 in. (5 cm.) wide. Bake for 25 to 30 minutes.

Remove from the oven onto a chopping board, and slice into thin pieces about ½-in. (1-cm.) wide using a serrated knife. Reduce the oven temperature to 300°F (150°C).

Lay the slices on the 2 baking sheets, and cook for a further 10 to 15 minutes. Turn over each slice and cook for a further 10 to 15 minutes, or until the slices are golden brown. Remove from the oven and allow to cool.

When cool, store in an airtight container. The cantucci will keep for a couple of weeks.

Makes 3 dozen

rum spice cookies

see variations page 320

Spicy rum cookies that taste great served with vanilla ice cream.

2 cups rolled oats
1½ cups all-purpose flour
1 scant cup coarsely ground almonds
1 tsp. ground cinnamon
½ tsp. ground allspice
½ tsp. ground ginger
1 tsp. baking powder

Pinch of salt
1 cup (2 sticks) sweet butter
1 cup superfine sugar
1 cup light brown sugar
2 eggs
2 tsp. rum flavor

Preheat the oven to 350°F (175°C). Line 2 baking sheets with parchment.

Combine the oats, flour, almonds, spices, baking powder, and salt and put to one side. Beat the butter and sugars until smooth. Add the eggs and rum and beat until blended. Stir in the dry ingredients.

Drop spoonfuls of batter about 1½ in. (4 cm.) apart on the baking sheets and bake 12 to 15 minutes. Transfer to a wire rack to cool. Store in an airtight container for 5 to 7 days.

Makes 3 dozen

lemon wafers

see variations page 321

Crisp lemon wafers are a refreshing accompaniment to ice creams or sorbets.

1 egg
½ cup superfine sugar
⅓ cup (¾ stick)sweet butter, melted
Grated zest of 1 lemon (2 to 3 tsp.)

Pinch of salt
1 cup plus 2 tbsp. all-purpose flour
Pinch of baking powder

Line 2 baking sheets with parchment. Beat the egg and sugar together in a mixing bowl, and stir in the melted butter, lemon zest, and salt. Sift the dry ingredients together and stir into the egg mixture. Cover and refrigerate the dough for 30 minutes.

Divide the dough in half. Roll each piece out between 2 plastic sheets or parchment to ¹⁄₁₆ in. (less than 2 mm.) thick. Refrigerate until firm. Preheat the oven to 400°F (200°C). Peel the top sheet from the dough and turn upside down. Peel off the second sheet. Use a 2½-in. (6¼-cm.) cookie cutter and place the cookies 1½ in. (4 cm.) apart on the baking sheets.

Bake for 6 to 8 minutes. Remove from the oven and lift the parchment to transfer the cookies to wire racks to cool.

When completely cool, store in an airtight container for 5 to 7 days.

Makes 2 dozen

caraway snaps

see variations page 322

Caraway is a wonderful spice — although it is less popular now than it was in the 16th century, when it was widely used to flavor cakes and cookies.

1 cup all-purpose flour
1¼ scant cups confectioners' sugar
3 egg whites

½ cup plus 2 tbsp. (1¼ sticks) sweet butter, melted
2 tbsp. caraway seeds

Line 2 baking sheets with parchment. Sift the flour and sugar together. Add the egg whites. Mix until smooth.

Stir in the melted butter and caraway seeds. Refrigerate the paste for 30 minutes.

Preheat the oven to 400°F (200°C).

Spread the paste in thin rounds about 3 in. (8 cm.) in diameter onto the baking sheets and bake for 4 to 5 minutes until golden. Remove from the baking sheets and shape over a rolling pin, or use wine bottles to give a more gradual curve to the cookie.

Store in an airtight container for 5 to 7 days.

Makes 3 dozen

amaretti

see variations page 323

These wonderful Italian cookies are great with coffee, or use them as a base to make Italian-style desserts.

1 tbsp. all-purpose flour
¾ cup confectioners' sugar
1¼ cups (6½ oz.) whole lightly toasted
    blanched almonds

3 egg whites
⅓ cup superfine sugar
1 tsp. grated lemon zest
1 tsp. almond extract

Preheat the oven to 275°F (140°C).

Sift the flour and confectioners' sugar together in a large bowl. Put the almonds in a food processor and blend until ground fine. Add them to the flour and sugar.

In a separate bowl, beat the egg whites to soft peaks, and beat in the superfine sugar one-third of the amount at a time. Add the lemon zest and almond extract.

Add half of the meringue to the dry ingredients and carefully add the remaining meringue. Using a piping bag and a ½-in. (1-cm.) nozzle, pipe the mixture into 1½-in. (4-cm.) rounds. Bake for 45 to 50 minutes until dry. If the amaretti start to brown, turn the oven temperature down. Remove from the oven and allow to cool. When completely cool, store in an airtight container for 1 to 2 weeks.

Makes 2 dozen

variations

langue de chat

see base recipe page 287

langue de chat with chocolate filling

Prepare and bake the basic cookie recipe and make up the chocolate filling.
Melt ¾ cup (4 oz.) bittersweet chocolate in a bowl over a pan of simmering
water, or in the microwave on a low setting. Boil ¼ cup of heavy cream in a
saucepan. Stir the cream into the chocolate until blended. Allow the filling
to cool slightly, and spread onto the bases of half the cookies. Sandwich
with the remaining halves. Store in an airtight container for 3 to 4 days.

palets des dames

Prepare the basic cookie dough and pipe small rounds of mixture onto the
baking sheets. Put 3 raisins on top of each round, and bake.

variations

french macaroons

see base recipe page 289

chocolate macaroons
Prepare the basic cookie dough and substitute 2 tablespoons Dutch
process cocoa powder for the pink food color. Sandwich the macaroons
together with chocolate-hazelnut spread.

mocha macaroons
Prepare the basic cookie dough and substitute 1 tablespoon instant
coffee powder for the pink food color. Sandwich together with chocolate-
hazelnut spread.

lemon macaroons
Prepare the basic cookie dough and substitute yellow food color for the pink
food color. Add the grated zest of 1 lemon (2 to 3 teaspoons). Sandwich the
macaroons together with apricot fruit preserve or lemon curd.

variations

brandy snaps

see base recipe page 290

cream-filled brandy snaps
Prepare the basic cookie dough and lightly whip 1 cup of heavy cream.
Add2 tablespoons superfine sugar and 1 teaspoon vanilla extract to the
cream. Use a piping bag and a ½ in. (1 cm.) nozzle to fill the brandy snaps
with cream. Fill each brandy snap from both ends to get an even distribution
of cream.

brandy snap baskets
Prepare the basic cookie dough and shape the warm cookies over small
bowls to make small baskets. Fill with ice cream and fresh fruit for
a quick summertime dessert.

variations

vanilla crescents

see base recipe page 293

lemon crescents
Prepare the basic cookie dough and substitute the grated zest of 1 lemon
(2 to 3 teaspoons) for the vanilla extract.

chocolate dipped vanilla crescents
Prepare the basic cookie dough and when the cookies are cool, half-dip
them in melted bittersweet chocolate.

hazelnut crescents
Prepare the basic cookie dough and substitute ground hazelnuts for
the ground almonds.

variations

sugared sablé

see base recipe page 294

raisin sablé
Prepare the basic cookie dough and add ½ cup raisins to the dough before shaping it into rolls.

walnut and cherry sablé
Prepare the basic cookie dough and substitute ½ cup ground walnuts for ½ cup of the flour. Add ½ cup (3 oz.) chopped candied red cherries to the dough before shaping it into rolls.

pistachio sablé
Prepare the basic cookie dough and substitute ½ cup (3 oz.) ground shelled pistachios for ½ cup of the flour. Add ½ cup (2 oz.) coarsely chopped pistachios to the dough before shaping it into rolls.

variations

brittle cookies

see base recipe page 295

brittle chocolate-orange cookies
Prepare the basic cookie dough and substitute Dutch process cocoa powder
for the instant coffee powder.

lemon vanilla brittle cookies
Prepare the basic cookie dough and substitute 2 teaspoons vanilla extract
for the instant coffee powder, and substitute lemon zest for the orange zest.

pistachio brittle cookies
Prepare the basic cookie dough and substitute Dutch process cocoa powder
for the instant coffee powder and pistachios for the hazelnuts.

variations

florentines

see base recipe page 297

ginger florentines
Prepare the basic cookie dough and substitute chopped candied ginger for
the candied peel.

hazelnut & cherry florentines
Prepare the basic cookie dough and substitute coarsely chopped hazelnuts
for the almonds and chopped green candied cherries for the candied lemon
and orange peel.

variations

boules de neige

see base recipe page 298

chocolate boules de neige
Prepare the basic cookie dough, adding 2 tablespoons sifted cocoa powder to the meringue with the coconut. Sandwich together with chocolate-hazelnut spread.

ginger boules de neige
Prepare the basic cookie dough and add 1 tablespoon (½ oz.) finely chopped candied ginger to the meringue with the coconut.

variations

orange almond tuiles

see base recipe page 301

coconut tuiles
Prepare the basic cookie dough and substitute 1¼ cups flaked coconut for
the almonds.

lemon and almond tuiles
Prepare the basic cookie dough and substitute lemon zest for the orange zest.

hazelnut tuiles
Prepare the basic cookie dough and substitute hazelnuts for the almonds
and ½ teaspoon ground cinnamon for the orange zest.

almond & lemon cantucci

see base recipe page 302

rosemary cantucci
Prepare the basic cookie dough and add 2 tablespoons chopped rosemary
to the dough with the nuts and the lemon.

fig & fennel cantucci
Prepare the basic cookie dough, but omit the lemon zest and add
2 teaspoons fennel seeds and 1 cup (5 oz.) chopped dried figs.

hazelnut & orange cantucci
Prepare the basic cookie dough and substitute toasted hazelnuts for the
almonds and orange zest for the lemon.

variations

rum spice cookies

see base recipe page 303

rum & raisin spice cookies
Prepare the basic cookie dough and add 1 cup (5 oz.) raisins.

rum, cherry, & coconut cookies
Prepare the basic cookie dough and substitute 1 heaped cup flaked coconut for the cup of oats. Add 1 cup (5 oz.) chopped red candied cherries.

rum & ginger cookies
Prepare the basic cookie dough and add 4 tablespoons (2 oz.) chopped candied ginger.

variations

lemon wafers

see base recipe page 304

lemon & poppy seed wafers
Prepare the basic cookie dough and add 1 tablespoon poppy seeds when
adding the dry ingredients.

cinnamon wafers
Prepare the basic cookie dough, but omit the lemon zest and add 1 teaspoon
ground cinnamon when adding the dry ingredients.

spicy wafers
Prepare the basic cookie dough and add 1 teaspoon ground cinnamon,
½ teaspoon ground ginger, and ½ teaspoon ground nutmeg when adding
the dry ingredients.

variations

caraway snaps

see base recipe page 307

chocolate caraway snaps
Prepare the basic cookie dough and add 2 tablespoons Dutch process cocoa powder to the dry ingredients.

pistachio snaps
Prepare the basic cookie dough, but omit the caraway seeds and before the cookie dough is baked, sprinkle it with finely chopped pistachio nuts.

lemon & ginger snaps
Prepare the basic cookie dough, but omit the caraway seeds. Add the grated zest of 2 lemons (5 to 6 teaspoons) and ½ teaspoon ground ginger.

variations

amaretti

see base recipe page 308

amaretti with rum
Prepare the basic cookie dough, but omit the lemon zest and almond extract
and add 1 tablespoon dark rum.

cherry amaretti
Prepare the basic cookie dough and add ½ cup (3 oz.) dried cherries.

soft amaretti
Prepare the basic cookie dough and bake the cookies at 350°F (175°C) for
12 to 15 minutes. When completely cool, store in an airtight container
for 5 to 7 days.

savory cookies & crackers

Cookies aren't always sweet — they are also perfect with cheese or accompanied by a sweet spread. From Scottish oatcakes to blue cheese crumbles and rosemary wafers, here are some fabulous savory cookies and crackers that should not be forgotten.

triple cheese sandwich cookies

see variations page 344

The ultimate cheesy cookie for those in need of a savory snack.

3 oz. mild cheddar cheese, grated
2 oz. sharp cheddar cheese, grated
2 oz. Parmesan cheese, grated
½ cup (1 stick) sweet butter

1 cup all-purpose flour
½ tsp. garlic salt
½ tsp. paprika
½ cup (4½ oz.) cream cheese

Line 2 baking sheets with parchment. Blend the cheeses and butter together.

Sift the flour, salt, and paprika together and stir into the butter and cheese mixture. Mix to form a soft dough. Shape the mixture into a 1½-in.- (4-cm.-) thick log. Wrap and refrigerate the dough for 15 minutes until firm.

Preheat the oven to 350°F (175°C). Cut the dough into ⅛-inch- (3-mm.-) thick slices. Place on baking sheets and bake for 10 to 12 minutes. Transfer to a wire rack to cool. When cool, spread half the cookie bases with cream cheese and then sandwich together with the remaining halves.

Store in an airtight container in the refrigerator for 1 to 2 days.

Makes 1½ dozen

cheese & pecan bites

see variations page 345

These savory cookies are a convenient snack to have on hand, and a great base for canapés if you're having a few friends over for a drink.

¼ cup (½ stick) sweet butter
4 oz. cheddar, grated
Pinch of cayenne pepper

Pinch of salt
¾ cup all-purpose flour
1 cup (3½ oz.) chopped pecans

Blend the butter and cheese together. Add the pepper, salt, and flour, and stir to form a smooth dough. Roll into a 2-in.- (5-cm.-) thick log, wrap and refrigerate the dough for 15 minutes until firm.

Preheat the oven to 350°F (175°C). Slice the dough into ¼-in.- (6-mm.-) thick pieces and place on baking sheets. Press pecans into the tops of each cookie and bake for 10 to 12 minutes until golden.

Transfer to a wire rack to cool. Store the cooled cookies in an airtight container for 5 to 7 days.

Makes 1 dozen

blue cheese crumbles

see variations page 346

Enjoy these cookies on their own or topped with a slice of your favorite cheese.

1¼ cups whole wheat flour
⅓ cup plus 2 tbsp. rolled oats
1 tbsp. light brown sugar
1½ tsp. baking powder
½ tsp. cayenne pepper

¼ tsp. salt
½ cup (1 stick) sweet butter
2 oz. blue cheese
2 to 3 tbsp. milk

Preheat the oven to 350°F (175°C). Line 2 baking sheets with parchment. Mix all the dry ingredients together in a bowl and cut in the butter. Crumble in half the blue cheese and add milk slowly to form a soft dough. Crumble the remaining cheese in a separate bowl and mix with the 2 tablespoons oats.

Roll out the dough on a lightly floured work surface to ⅛ in. (3 mm.) thick and cut out rounds using a 2½-in. (6.5-cm.) cutter. Place the cookies on a baking sheet. Brush the cookies with water and lightly press the reserved cheese and oats on top of the cookies. Bake for 15 to 20 minutes until golden.

Remove from the oven. Place onto a wire rack and allow to cool. When completely cool, store in an airtight container for 3 to 4 days.

Makes 1 dozen

savory nut cookies

see variations page 347

You'll simply love these unusual savory nut cookies — the perfect accompaniment to your after-dinner coffee.

1 cup (2 sticks) sweet butter
8 oz. grated cheddar cheese
2 cups all-purpose flour

½ tsp. salt
½ cup (2 oz.) chopped pecans
1½ cups crisped rice cereal

Preheat the oven to 350°F (175°C). Line 2 baking sheets with parchment.

Mix the butter and cheese together. Stir in the flour and salt, and add the pecans and crisped rice cereal. Roll the mixture into small balls and place on the baking sheets. Flatten with the back of a fork dipped in water. Bake for 10 to 12 minutes.

Remove from the oven, transfer to wire racks, and cool. Store in an airtight container for 3 to 4 days.

Makes 3 dozen

chili cheese thins

see variations page 348

Hot and spicy wafer-thin cookies are great to nibble while enjoying a pre-dinner drink.

2 cups all-purpose flour
½ tsp. baking powder
1 cup (2 sticks) sweet butter

Pinch of hot chili powder
4 oz. Parmesan, finely grated

Preheat the oven to 350°F (175°C). Line 2 baking sheets with parchment. Sift the flour and baking powder together and cut in the butter until the mixture resembles breadcrumbs. Then add the chili powder and Parmesan and continue working the dough until it comes together.

Roll out the dough between 2 sheets of parchment to 1/16 in. (less than 2 mm.) thick. Remove the top layer of parchment and cut the dough into 4 in. (10 cm.) lengths ½ in. (1 cm.) wide. Prick the dough lightly. Re-roll any leftover dough.

Place the cookies onto baking sheets and bake 8 to 10 minutes until golden. Lift the parchment and transfer to wire racks.

When completely cool, store in an airtight container for 5 to 7 days.

Makes 2 dozen

oatcakes

see variations page 349

These savory oat biscuits are simple but delicious topped with your favorite savory spread.

2 cups fine oatmeal
$\frac{1}{4}$ tsp. baking soda
$\frac{1}{4}$ tsp. salt

1 tbsp. lard
1$\frac{1}{4}$ cups water

Preheat the oven to 350°F (175°C). Line 2 baking sheets with parchment.

Mix the oatmeal, baking soda, and salt together in a bowl. Gently heat the lard and water in a small pan until the lard has melted and add enough of the liquid to make a firm dough.

Roll out the dough onto an oatmeal-covered surface to $\frac{1}{8}$ in. (3 mm.) thick and cut out cookies using a round cutter, or cut into wedges if you prefer.

Place the oatcakes on baking sheets and bake 12 to 15 minutes. Transfer to a wire rack to cool. Store in an airtight container for 5 to 7 days.

Makes 2 dozen

lemon & black pepper butter biscuits

see variations page 350

Spicy, buttery, melt-in-the-mouth biscuits.

1½ cups all-purpose flour, sifted
½ cup (1 stick) sweet butter
1 tsp. grated lemon zest

½ tsp. freshly ground black pepper
1 egg
2 tsp. rock salt

Preheat the oven to 350°F (175°C). Line 2 baking sheets with parchment.

Cut the butter into the flour until the mixture resembles fine breadcrumbs. Add the lemon zest and black pepper, and then the egg. Mix to form a stiff dough.

Roll out the dough onto a lightly floured surface to ⅛ in. (3 mm.) thick. Cut out the dough with a cutter of your choice. Transfer the dough to a baking sheet. Brush with egg white and sprinkle with rock salt.

Bake for 10 minutes or until golden. Cool on a wire rack and store in an airtight container for 5 to 7 days.

Makes 2 dozen

anchovy & olive sticks

see variations page 351

Tip: If the dough of this recipe is too stiff, add water; if it's too wet, simply add flour.

2 tsp. dried active yeast
1½ cups warm water
3½ cups bread flour
2 tsp. granulated sugar

1 tsp. salt
4 tsp. olive oil
3 tbsp. chopped anchovies
3 tbsp. chopped black olives

Preheat the oven to 400°F (200°C). Line 2 baking sheets and sprinkle with semolina. Whisk together the yeast and water and stir in 1⅔ cups flour and the sugar. Cover and leave in a warm place for 20 minutes. Put the remaining flour in the bowl of a food processor and add the salt, 2 teaspoons olive oil, and the starter dough. Mix with the dough hook for 5 to 10 minutes.

Put the dough into a large oiled bowl, brush the top of the dough with 1 teaspoon olive oil, and cover with plastic wrap. Leave in a warm place until doubled in size. Flatten the dough on a floured work surface and gently press in anchovies and olives. Roll out the dough with a rolling pin. If the dough shrinks back, cover it with a clean tea towel and allow to rest for 10 minutes. Roll the dough out to ½ in. (1 cm.) thick and rest it again.

Roughly cut the dough into ½ in. (1 cm.) strips, transfer them to the baking sheets, and brush them with the remaining olive oil. Rest them in a warm place for 10 to 15 minutes and then bake for 12 to 15 minutes. They are best eaten on the day they are made.

Makes 2 dozen

rosemary wafers

see variations page 352

Herby little cookies that are great served as an accompaniment to dips or pâte.

2 cups all-purpose flour
½ tsp. baking powder
¾ cup (1½ sticks) sweet butter
Pinch of salt

3 oz. Parmesan, finely grated
2 tbsp. freshly chopped rosemary
2 egg yolks

Preheat the oven to 350°F (175°C). Line 2 baking sheets with parchment. Mix the flour and baking powder together, and cut in the butter until the mixture resembles breadcrumbs. Add the Parmesan, rosemary, and egg yolks, and continue working the dough until it comes together.

Roll out the dough on a lightly floured surface to ⅛ in. (3 mm.) thick and cut into squares. Place the cookies onto baking sheets and bake 8 to 10 minutes until golden.

Lift the parchment and transfer to wire racks. When completely cool, store in an airtight container for 5 to 7 days.

Makes 2 dozen

water biscuits

see variations page 353

Traditional savory biscuits that are ever so simple to make.

¾ cup all-purpose flour
Pinch of salt
2 tbsp. water
2 tbsp. (¼ stick) butter

Preheat the oven to 400°F (200°C). Line 2 baking sheets with parchment.

Sift the flour and salt together in a bowl. Put the water and butter in a small pan and heat gently until the butter has melted. Add the liquid to the flour and mix to a smooth dough.

Roll the dough out thinly on a lightly floured work surface. Cut the dough out using a 3-in. (8-cm.) cutter. Place onto baking sheets and prick with a fork.

Bake for 12 to 15 minutes until crisp and golden. Cool on a wire rack and store in an airtight container for up to 2 weeks.

Makes 1½ dozen

mustard & cream cheese sandwich biscuits

see variations page 354

Crispy, crunchy, and very addictive, these snack biscuits are a personal favorite.

1¼ cups all-purpose flour
½ tsp. mustard powder
¼ cup (½ stick) sweet butter
3 oz. cheddar cheese, grated

¾ cup (6 oz.) crunchy peanut butter
1 egg
¾ cup (6¾ oz.) cream cheese

Preheat the oven to 350°F (175°C). Sift flour and mustard powder together. Cut in the butter until the mixture resembles breadcrumbs. Stir in cheese, then add the peanut butter and the egg and mix to a smooth paste.

Roll out the dough on a lightly floured surface to ¼ in. (6 mm.) thick. Cut out the dough using a 2-in. (5-cm.) cutter and place the shapes on the baking sheets.

Bake for 10 to 12 minutes until golden. Transfer to a wire rack to cool. Beat the cream cheese to soften it. Spread it on the bases of half the cookies and sandwich together with the remaining cookie halves.

Store in an airtight container in the refrigerator for 2 to 3 days.

Makes 2 dozen

twice-baked walnut & raisin finger cookies

see variations page 355

Savory fruit and nut biscotti that are great served with cheese or simply eaten on their own as a late-night snack.

¼ cup (½ stick) sweet butter	½ cup (2 oz.) ground walnuts
3 eggs	½ cup cornmeal
1 cup all-purpose flour	1 cup (5 oz.) raisins
½ tsp. baking powder	½ cup (2 oz.) chopped walnuts

Preheat the oven to 350°F (175°C). Grease and flour 2 baking sheets. Beat the butter and eggs until well blended. Then add the flour, baking powder, ground walnuts, and cornmeal. Stir to mix then add the raisins and chopped walnuts and mix to a smooth paste.

Divide the dough between the baking sheets and shape into 2 flat loaves about 10 in. (25.5 cm.) long and 2 in. (5 cm.) wide. Bake 20 minutes until pale golden and dry. Remove from the oven onto a chopping board and slice into thin pieces about ¼ to ½ in. (0.5 to 1 cm.) wide using a serrated knife. Lay the slices baking on the baking sheets and cook for a further 10 to 15 minutes, then turn over each slice and cook for a further 10 to 15 minutes or until the slices are golden brown. Remove from the oven and allow to cool. When stored in an airtight container, the cookies will keep for a couple of weeks.

Makes 3 dozen

triple cheese sandwich cookies

see base recipe page 325

triple cheese cookies with blue cheese filling
Prepare the basic cookie recipe. When the cookies are cool, mix 2 oz. blue cheese with the cream cheese and use to sandwich the cookies together.

walnut-crusted triple cheese cookies
Prepare the basic cookie dough. Before baking the cookies, press ½ cup (2 oz.) chopped walnuts into the cookie dough. Omit the cream cheese and do not sandwich together.

poppy seed & cheese cookies
Prepare the basic cookie dough, substituting mild cheddar for the sharp cheddar and Parmesan cheeses and adding 1 tablespoon poppy seeds to the dough.

variations

cheese & pecan bites

see base recipe page 327

cheese & macadamia cookies
Prepare the basic cookie dough and substitute macadamias for the pecans.

oaty cheese & pecan cookies
Prepare the basic cookie dough and substitute 2 tablespoons oats for
2 tablespoons flour.

walnut, cheese, & raisin cookies
Prepare the basic cookie dough. Add ¼ cup (2 oz.) raisins to the dough and
substitute walnuts for the pecans.

variations

blue cheese crumbles

see base recipe page 328

blue cheese & pecan crumbles
Prepare the basic cookie dough and substitute 2 tablespoons chopped pecans for 2 tablespoons oats.

blue cheese & raisin crumbles
Prepare the basic cookie dough and add ¼ cup (2 oz.) raisins to the dough after adding the milk.

blue cheese & date crumbles
Prepare the basic cookie dough and add ¼ cup (2 oz.) chopped dates to the dough after adding the milk.

variations

savory nut cookies

see base recipe page 331

walnut, date, & blue cheese cookies
Prepare the basic cookie dough. Substitute blue cheese for half the cheddar, walnuts for the pecans, and add ½ cup (3 oz.) finely chopped dates.

macadamia cookies
Prepare the basic cookie dough and substitute macadamias for the pecans.

mixed nut cookies
Prepare the basic cookie dough. Substitute ½ cup (2 oz.) chopped peanuts for ½ cup crisped rice-cereal.

variations

chili cheese thins

see base recipe page 332

chili cheese thins with peanuts
Prepare the basic cookie recipe. Before baking, brush the cookies with a little milk and sprinkle with 1 tablespoon chopped peanuts.

double decker cheese thins
Prepare the basic cookie recipe and sandwich the cookies together with cream cheese or peanut butter.

mustard cheese thins
Prepare the basic cookie dough, substituting ¼ teaspoon mustard powder for the chili powder.

variations

oatcakes

see base recipe page 333

sesame oatcakes
Prepare the basic cookie dough and add 2 tablespoons sesame seeds to
the dry ingredients.

griddled oatcakes
Prepare the basic cookie dough and instead of baking the cookies, cook
them on a griddle pan for 6 to 8 minutes. They will curl up at little at the
edges to give a more uneven appearance.

black pepper oatcakes
Prepare the basic cookie dough and add 2 teaspoons coarsely ground black
pepper to the dry ingredients.

variations

lemon & black pepper butter biscuits

see base recipe page 334

oregano & lemon butter biscuits
Prepare the basic cookie dough and substitute dried oregano for the
black pepper.

caraway butter biscuits
Prepare the basic cookie dough. Omit the black pepper and substitute
caraway seeds for the rock salt.

sun-dried tomato butter biscuits
Prepare the basic cookie dough. Omit the black pepper and lemon and
add 1 tablespoon chopped sun-dried tomatoes to the dough.

variations

anchovy & olive sticks

see base recipe page 337

black & green olive sticks
Prepare the basic cookie dough and substitute green olives for the anchovies.

tomato & rosemary sticks
Prepare the basic cookie dough. Substitute chopped sun-dried tomatoes and chopped fresh rosemary for the anchovies and olives.

parmesan sticks
Prepare the basic cookie dough, omitting the anchovies and olives and adding 3 oz. finely grated Parmesan to the dough. Sprinkle the sticks with Parmesan after brushing with olive oil.

variations

rosemary wafers

see base recipe page 338

thyme wafers
Prepare the basic cookie dough and substitute thyme for the rosemary.

walnut & rosemary cookies
Prepare the basic cookie dough and substitute ½ cup (2 oz.) ground walnuts for ½ cup of the flour.

goat cheese & rosemary cookies
Prepare the basic cookie dough and substitute ¼ cup soft goat's cheese for the Parmesan.

variations

water biscuits

see base recipe page 340

bubble biscuits
Prepare the basic cookie recipe. Cut out the biscuits and place them on the baking sheets but do not prick them with a fork. When baked they will bubble.

caraway water biscuits
Prepare the basic cookie recipe. Put the cookies on the baking sheets. After pricking them, brush with water and sprinkle with 1 tablespoon caraway seeds.

salt & pepper water biscuits
Prepare the basic cookie recipe. Put the cookies on the baking sheets. After pricking them, brush with water and sprinkle with rock salt and freshly ground black pepper.

variations

mustard & cream cheese sandwich biscuits

see base recipe page 341

mustard & blue cheese sandwich biscuits
Prepare the basic cookie dough, adding 2 oz. blue cheese to the cream cheese for the biscuit filling.

mustard, cream cheese, & onion sandwich biscuits
Prepare the basic cookie dough, adding 3 finely chopped scallions to the cream cheese for the biscuit filling.

pecan & cream cheese sandwich biscuits
Prepare the basic cookie dough, omitting the mustard and adding ½ cup (2 oz.) chopped pecans to the dough.

variations

twice-baked walnut & raisin finger cookies

see base recipe page 342

twice-baked walnut & cranberry finger cookies
Prepare the basic cookie dough and substitute dried cranberries for
the raisins.

twice-baked hazelnut & raisin finger cookies
Prepare the basic cookie dough and substitute hazelnuts for the walnuts.

twice-baked walnut & date finger cookies
Prepare the basic cookie dough and substitute chopped dates for the raisins.

index

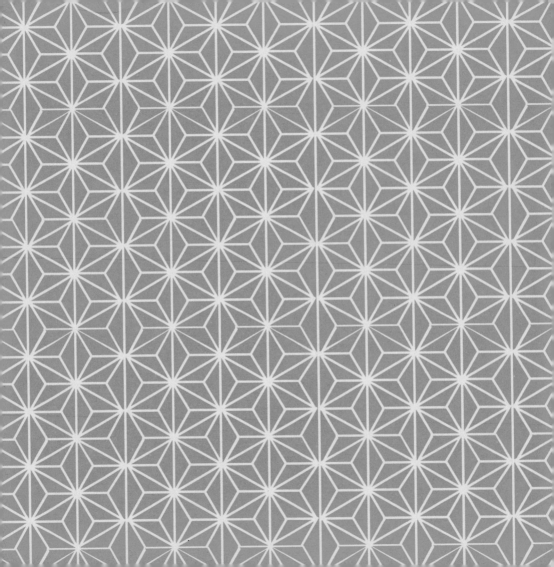